While I Was Walking

by

Sally Russo

PublishAmerica
Baltimore

First printing

ISBN: 1-4241-5818-4
PUBLISHED BY PUBLISHAMERICA, LLLP
www.publishamerica.com
Baltimore

Printed in the United States of America

For Mom and Dad, thank you.

Intro

I have tasted the salt in the air, breathed the calm wind that sweeps off the southern shore embracing my face. Against the blue sky that has been painted above me lies the sweet remains of souls that have danced bravely on this very same earth. The clouds so boldly hang among our eyes to be viewed and then simply cast away. Some leave an impression in our minds making for a moment a permanent grave in our own world. Others we carelessly disregard as they gently pass us by. My eyes gaze beyond the clouds to a reflection below. The water is rough today, waves that seem angry at life or disturbed enough to be heard by those around. I am the only one there to hear their cries reach the shore, so I try desperately to listen.

This vast mystery is such an endless journey to me. This ocean of time, life, travel, history, memories and most of all beauty; to know its thoughts would truly be heroic. For years now I have come to this very shore. I come seeking solitude, adventure, prayer, answers, guidance and sanctity. A moment at ease to release my own crazed thoughts from a world thus traveled. Far beneath that great carpet of water lies the answers I have vainly sought for such a long time. If only God could hear me and wash them upon this shore, that golden sand that rolls out before me with such piety and grandeur. Occasionally I see a small token and treasure that I find worth keeping, a small piece of the world that has voyaged through that very ocean to reach the breast of this land. I embrace it and hold it graciously in my hands. I wonder too often where this tiny shell has been, the things it has encountered, and the life it has endured. To be such an intricate part of something so much greater in size and depth, does it feel lost?

This shell of such lightly tinted hues that seem to shine when brought into the sunlight. For a moment I feel myself in this shell. There I remain so small a treasure of life in such a vast world of indifference, hardships, triumphs and secrets. I have been on voyages and journeys only to be washed back upon the same shore and battling the same fights. It is a difficult force that drives me back here to the sands I so badly want to call home. But yet my time at sea has not reached its final mission at heart, there is still "work to be had on the ocean" before I can find myself on land. Like that small shell I have felt lost at times beneath the walls around me which engulf my soul. Drowning at times I have fought wars only to be left uneasy, heartbroken or alone. Sunken in the sands of nature and fate I have remained alive and afloat in spite of all that has taken my breath. A new shore has been on the horizon, as I swim towards it, I see the sun dancing over the dunes. So beautiful a sight to envision; a new land, a new future, a possible answer. I only pray to be placed softly in its palms.

As I see that ocean every day, it is still as though I am feeling and looking upon it for the first time. I hope never to take its beauty, mystery and power for granted; so let me bathe in it, swim until I drown and forever live for the shore to appear. With that in mind I prepare to reveal myself, bare my truth, and live as I do now in the moment changing with the tides and casting away to the seas. There are moments, seconds, minutes and even years I see myself in that ocean. So solemn and strong, overpowering and leaving behind the marks of my beliefs with each coast I encounter and crash upon. However, for each of those moments I do have days, weeks and months where I feel as though I am that small shell of life dispersed among the sea in a miserable army of confusion and terror. I want so badly to elude those feelings and encompass all that this great ocean has to offer.

So now I pray, make me a ship, a creature that feels both the power and fear of the sea while journeying through it, set out for challenges and land to conquer. Let me sail about the world with the wind at my back and my dreams in my heart, it is this that I call the adventure; it is this that I call life.

***

Growing up I lived off a busy street; well, actually, sometimes it was busy. Living in a tourist area has its benefits and definite downfalls. On Cape Cod we experience sheer pandemonium from about May until September. Then, just like that, all sleeps quietly among the calming waves. Aside from the occasional holiday weekend or screaming getaway, the fall, winter and spring become the local's time to breathe.

When you spend every waking minute of your youth in a place like this, of course you only grow to despise it. I could not wait to get away from it all. I always loved the thought of starting a new life somewhere else. But like all things that come full circle I would eventually grow to love and appreciate this place I called home. In fact it became the only real place I could go that seemed to make life's worries dissipate even just for a moment. Isn't that always the case though, like children when we feel afraid or challenged in our lives, we have a tendency to run and flock home to the place we once lived life so innocently. We tend to escape and hide when things seem too tough to face head on or simply when we need to look at things from a different perspective. For me the Cape will always be that place. It is my childhood, my sanity, and my peace. In fact that is why it only seemed fair to write this book from the confines of my comfort place, my home.

Chapter 1

All my life I have been running, in many ways that can be said in both a physical and literal sense. Well, more recently it has become more literal than anything. As a child it was more physical. Stopping for merely nothing I found my solace when I was running and playing any sport.

Being the youngest in a family with two older sisters I suppose my overexposure to the daily athletic events had me hooked. Still, I felt I had shadows cast upon my face from the accomplishments my two sisters had so valiantly achieved. I wanted my own name, an opportunity to step into my own instead of simply being the youngest of a family of three athletes. Not that I was ashamed to bear that name, I just wanted to be seen for my own ability. So I wasted no time finding my sports and excelling to my fullest potential. It made me feel alive and invincible. So with my dreams at heart I made a promise to myself to simply "play" as long as possible. It is a funny thing with dreams – almost as if they have no negative limits or twists to them, I suppose that is why they will always be called dreams.

At the time I was blinded by only what I loved, and I never imagined anyone taking that away from me. I didn't have much to show for in the classroom, that part was always a struggle; but when it came to sports, I could always perform in a way I never could with anything else. I loved the thrill of playing in front of a crowded field or court with my family and friends watching me. It was a chance to show what I could do. But I was biased in my fan base and did have one favorite in particular, my grandfather, and he was always my biggest fan. There was an unexplainable feeling that would overcome me when I saw him walking down to see me play. I would see him walking across the fields, his frail body fighting any weather just to see me compete. I thought if he could make it across those fields at his age then I could win that game for him that day. So I always made that my goal before each game. I played to make him proud. He never missed a game and I loved him for that, he was my true inspiration.

When my grandmother passed away in 1991, I developed a special connection with my grandfather. They had been married for fifty-three years when she passed from a stroke on July 3, 1991. It was that day I saw for the first time a piece of my grandfather buried as well. He was always so sad to me after that. Luckily he only lived three houses away so he practically lived at my parent's house. When my older sisters, Ann and Elizabeth, went away to school and it was just myself at home, I felt my grandfather shed his "grand" title and became more of a father to me. I felt blessed to have two amazing father figures in my life. He was filled with all kinds of advice for me. Whether it was about love, work, wealth or simply family. His words always left a permanent place in my soul. To have known true love was to have known my grandparents. They celebrated their marriage and life together in so many ways. I knew him living without her by his side were the most challenging years of his life. But he did and I vowed to always live the same. For five years he fought until he was taken from us in April of 1996.

I knew that day he was now at peace in the arms of my grandmother, but I would miss him dearly. I paid my respects by giving the eulogy at his funeral. It was the most difficult thing I ever had to do, but I felt I owed him that. At the cemetery I was embraced by something I had once heard from a priest and always remember when someone passes away. He spoke of life and how when we are born we are each given a bag of seeds. As we grow and experience things, we plant these seeds along with us. Then as our last breath is taken and we are put to rest, we can leave behind a beautiful garden for people to remember us by.

My grandfather would no longer show his presence on the sidelines, but I knew every game he was there in spirit. I knew he saw my accomplishments and would have been proud of me and the future I had set before me. Everyone would miss him on the sidelines. My coaches and teammates all knew him and loved the support he brought to the field.

I remember one field hockey practice I lost the gold cross pendant my grandfather had given me for Christmas and I had worn ever since. Everyone knew its sentimental value to me; so just like that, the next thing I knew, we were all on the ground pacing through the grass searching for this chain and pendant. With him gone it was something that always made me feel so close to him while I was playing. It was as though his spirit ran with me out on that field. We never did find the necklace that day or any day after. In my dream world I always imagined that some young child had found it and had kept it with them as a good luck charm. Or maybe somehow, someday, it would just find its way back to me. But that's me and just my over the top beliefs in fate. Still I never stopped looking for the necklace and probably never will, that's just a fact.

Still without my grandfather there I wanted to work even harder because I knew he would have wanted me to. I spent the majority of my senior year deterring colleges I felt no interest in and accepting invitations to visit the one's that truly appealed to me on a different level...athletics. School to me was never anything but a chore. It really got in the way of what my real passion was all about. I admit it, I was a jock and still deeply am at heart. Some kids are known for their brains, some their artistic sense, some their quirkiness, some their ability to always seem in the wrong place at the wrong time and then there are those, like myself, who are known best for their love of competition. But my dreams became a reality and success when I reached my senior year and had colleges knocking at my door. By December I had narrowed my choice to a large college out in Michigan and a school in the western part of Massachusetts. Both had their strong points and were both highly competitive field hockey teams, and both had offered to pay for my entire education for four years as well. It was a grueling decision that needed to be made by December 20th.

Field hockey was my addiction, my passion, and my drive. I saw college simply as the next route to getting to play this sport at an even higher and more intense level. Class would simply be a way to pass the time between practice and games. So maybe my entire perspective was a bit skewed, but still I was getting a free education for my insane thinking.

I tied up all my loose ends around home only to reach my graduation day on June 7, 1997. It was that day I not only walked before my family and friends to accept my diploma, but I began my walk towards the next real challenge in my life. High school was finally at an end, and I was about to embark upon a whole new journey, college bound to a university in western Massachusetts.

I chose my destination purely on field hockey. At the time the college in Massachusetts was about tenth in the country and the coach was very well-respected. With my heart set on eventually playing for our country, I figured I could not go wrong by finding guidance in the hands of our own countries coach. My plan backfired when she decided to leave and focus on the Olympic team just months before I was to start the season. My heart was broken but still I forged ahead with my goals in sight. After all she had recruited me and given me a full scholarship to come to her team at the time. It was simply just a minor bump in the road that I felt I would overcome.

I spent the days of my last summer that year training and working, with the occasional night spent among old friends and familiar faces that I knew would soon be gone. As the summer dwindled to a closing, I found my excitement transforming to fear. I was afraid for the first time in awhile. I guess things always seem easier when they are months away from actually happening. However, I managed to pack up my room and personal things in August and head off to college to venture into that new beginning I had so vastly awaited. The car ride seemed quick knowing I was merely moments away from being on my own and getting my first real chance to escape the comforts of home and family.

Every once in awhile there comes a time in our lives when we just know we will never forget how we feel. That was one of them. I remember standing for a moment hugging my parents and then, just like that, watching them drive off into the distance. It is such a sad feeling literally watching the distance between you and loved ones grow before you. Still I will never forget that feeling from that day. Though I have done it a million times since there is something unexplainable the first time it occurs to you that you really are alone.

Chapter 2

Being a part of an athletic team has its good and bad sides. The bad being you must arrive at school two and a half weeks earlier than the other students, the good is the instant friendships you gain from your twenty some-odd teammates. For myself, I kept quiet at first just getting used to the idea of all these new people in my life. However, it did not take long to let them know me and where I came from. It wasn't long before these strangers became a family and group of even familiar faces to me.

Nobody really prepares you for that when you go to school. Nobody sits you down and tells you how the people you meet at school become different kinds of friends because they know you under such different circumstances. Unlike the friends we have in high school these people truly see you in all stages of your life. They are home with you at night, they get up with you in the morning, they eat with you, they are up with you when you cannot sleep; in many ways you are becoming a part of a larger family. It can be a saving grace in a large school to find those few people who you can consider your family. I came to realize this unfortunately the hard way, but more importantly at least I realized it.

My freshman year was mainly consumed by field hockey. The schedule was demanding and challenging but served rewarding at all costs. It was definitely not an easy transition from high school to college but with time I adjusted and held my own on the field. The classroom on the other hand was a different story. But I did what I needed to skim by and continue playing through the fall season, which came to an end in November at the NCAA tournament. We placed 9th in the country for Division I after losing a close game, but more importantly, I had achieved something greater – my respect among my teammates both on and off the field. Not a bad start for my first collegiate year. I could not believe I was actually a starter on a Division I team, I only hoped my grandfather was looking down upon me, I know he would have been so proud of that.

As the field hockey season concluded, I found my time much more available for more of the freshman activities. The typical drinking and socialization that most students experience in the first month were now readily available to the team as we were no longer under the "No Drinking" policy. We wasted no time at all in catching up to our fellow students. I began spending my time with the older girls on the team. For some reason they took a liking to me which allowed me to escape from the campus dorm life when necessary. Over time those small dorm rooms can become a bit confining to the mind. So I was grateful to escape at any time possible.

I became a little sister to those girls on the team and all their friends. Caitlin was a junior on the team and more of a sister to me than anyone at the school. She never hesitated to pick me up and take me out of those small cell walls I called home. I knew and met more people in that one semester than I had in my whole life at that point. I started to find myself in this new world, and I was finding a side of myself I had never known, I felt untouchable.

If only I could have stayed in that moment of ecstasy forever. Unfortunately life does not operate solely around our good fortune, each day does have to begin and each day does have to end. But still I had emerged from the shadows of my sister's accomplishments to create my own achievements and to finally stand proud amongst my own spotlight. The scariest and saddest part of that moment occurred when the spotlight slowly faded, and I found myself standing in the dark faced with a new challenge and a face I could no longer look at or recognize in the mirror.

Chapter 3

As a child I once felt fearless. I saw the world through the simple colors, which I painted in my own mind. Unbeknownst I had no idea it would become almost a parallel to the reality I would face in the years to come. Beyond my childish imagination I felt I was invincible. I can distinctly remember my mother telling me the truth as well as the harsh cruelties that I would most likely encounter. She did her job of forewarning me of those around me and the value of trust. Her words echoed loudly in my head for many years. She prepared me about friends and how some may not remain true forever, she spoke gently about my heart and how it would open with passion and fall in pain, she praised about family and the importance of the morals and values we shared; however through all she spoke, nothing could have prepared me for my own fate.

The night air had never seemed so long and cold. I wrapped my arms tightly around my lifeless body struggling to find the rhythm of my own heart, but all that remained was the constant lull of fear. My body remained the empty vessel of something untold and I was scared. I saw nothing before me but the shallow existence of a place I did not want to be, I'd never been more alone. After what felt like hours, I had reached my destination, a small dorm room decorated among its own virginal passions. Quietly opening the door I felt in a trance, my eyes fixed on the red numbers of the digital clock, which read 5:30 am. How could it be? Four hours melted from my memory, yet not one moment would be forgotten. I knew it would become something permanently branded in the depths of my own nightmares. I curled into a ball and cried myself to sleep, silently hoping to never awake again. An innocent night turned so guilty, I knew I would never be the same.

On November 23, 1997 I became another statistic another number so to speak. Like so many of the others out there I now felt destined to become another after school special. I was eighteen years old and soon to grow up much faster. Four football players at the university had raped me; I suddenly felt my life take a quick turn. Three of the boys were students at the university, the other was a former student who had transferred to a college in California and was just in town visiting.

It started out as a normal Saturday night, the gathering of friends and overindulgence of alcohol. Some of the girls and I got together for a night of just pure, and what should have been, innocent fun. By the early morning hours we were at a house party. I was tired and ready to go home. My friends set me up with a ride with some of their friends on the football team. I knew them all well and was more than comfortable leaving with them than anyone else there. By the time we reached the dorms some of us decided to go and hang out for a little longer. I regained some energy at that point and agreed to that.

I missed my guy friends from home and enjoyed the company of a relaxed atmosphere. My sisters and I always were the type of girls who had more male friends than female. Maybe it was partly due to the athletic background or just our disinterest in the petty gossip that existed among a room full of girls. Still nonetheless I was comfortable. Some would say I was just naive, stupid or even too drunk to care. But to this day I would still go back and take that same ride home from them that night. What I didn't expect was the inevitable. I never expected them to turn on me; I never expected something so innocent among friends to change so quickly.

I suddenly felt weak, sick and could hardly keep my mind focused. I felt I was thrown into a different world. I had no words, no strength and no energy to do anything. I felt as though I was the smallest most lifeless form ever to walk the earth. My fear engulfed my mind and I froze. I was probably half the size of one of the boys and there were four of them there. How could I fight? My memory still cannot piece those four hours together. I remember only flashes of fear and my still dead body. It was as though I was somewhere else. I don't think I will ever know if that was the alcohol, terror or something beyond my control that erased my memory from that night. Had I been drugged? Had I passed out or was I just so terrified I mentally escaped somewhere far away? I still have never uncovered the answer to this burning question and I know I probably never will.

Looking back maybe I would have found the strength to do something but at the time I feared anyone telling me this was my fault and I should have done something different. I knew I could never relay that fear into anyone's mind and no matter what anyone says they would never really know what to do unless they were put in that exact situation, so I didn't want to be judged for my lack of actions. I felt nobody could understand or give advice on the situation because they simply would not understand my mind or my thinking. I have played that night a million times over in my head and wish I could have fought or done something differently, but I soon realized that was never going to change. How it happened would never change, how I dealt with it would never change, the only thing capable of changing was myself.

I suppose the most difficult part of my experience was trying to cope with the after effects. At the time I knew of only one quick and instant remedy for my pain, alcohol.

The solution seemed perfect at the time; whenever I felt discomfort, simple, numb the pain. So this is what I did. At first it was the answer to all of my minds crazed thoughts. I felt at fault for what had happened so in many ways I took this upon myself as my own form of imprisonment.

The following week was Thanksgiving, and I had not been home since I left that August. Instead of anxiously packing my things and getting out of town for five days, I decided only to go home for one night and leave early Friday morning. Sarah was a friend of my sister's who ended up working at the college and so the two of us headed to my parents to spend the holiday. I had not known her very long but we had an instant connection. But I found myself even too afraid to talk to her so I hid the truth and buried my face for the next twenty-four hours. I felt too ashamed to bear my face in front of my family, it was so sad to see how much had changed since I had last been home.

I had felt like they would see what had happened to me just by looking at me and blame me for drinking or not taking action. I sat quietly at home where I had been so innocent all my life and now feeling at fault. That night at home was one of the most difficult nights of my life. As I lay in my bed awake, I was embarrassed, afraid and distant. I felt so far from reality and all I wanted to do was to just go back in time to somewhere more childlike. I curled myself in my bed and fought away the nightmare that poisoned my brain trying desperately to answer my own questions. Looking back I will never know what my family was really thinking that Thanksgiving day. I only hope I somehow have made them understand my actions and my fear that lived so loudly within me at that time.

When I returned back to school, I had arranged to stay at Caitlin and the other girls house on the team. When Caitlin had heard what happened to me she said nothing except, "I am coming to get you." She did not want me to be alone and definitely did not want me on that campus where everything had taken place. She felt so bad and guilty because they were her friends who did this to me. I will never know what must have gone through her head when she heard her good friends, who she had gone to school with for two years and been friends with, could do this to someone she cared about. It was hard for me to even tell her that it was them and what they had done. All those girls were experiencing the same things...a betrayal from friends. I wanted so badly for it to not be true. Again I was feeling guilty that I had ruined their friendships. My guilt ran deep and those days I spent alone I was wishing I had never said anything to anyone about that night. The house was a shelter from reality, and I wished I could stay there forever. That was the only Thanksgiving break I would stay anywhere alone. Those few days seemed like an eternity as I battled my own war in my head.

As the break neared an end, I was haunted of the thought of everyone coming back to school. Though I thought I was at peace in my solitude, I was probably just too drunk and alone to realize anything at all. Still I knew I liked that feeling of isolation, it was the only time I could feel guilt without having to actually look at anyone and feel worse about myself. I will always be thankful to those girls who let me stay in their house that Thanksgiving without asking any questions, just opening their hearts and door to me. I knew at the time everyone probably had their own questions for me and why I wanted to be so alone after something so horrible, but still they never asked, not even when they returned home.

I stopped going to class in those following weeks in fear of who I may see, or even worse, in fear of how I would be seen. I sheltered myself to those small cell walls of my dorm room. I slept all day, and when my mind was not at ease dreaming, I calmed my fears by drinking. Although it never stopped at just one, eventually that one led to an endless consistency of poison. I had only four weeks left in the semester before Christmas break so I found this behavior to be the only possible way to remain sane and not have to drop out and lose all the work I had completed up to that point.

My hours of stupidity grew longer as I drowned my own sober days into the past. The days and nights slowly faded together as time no longer seemed a factor in the present moments of my mind. I was in one of three states each day: drunk, hung over or asleep. Somehow nothing else seemed to matter; I shut out anyone familiar to my conscious state of mind to find at most times I was alone. Slowly I watched my identity fade into a shadowed memory. By the close of the semester, I packed up for Christmas break but with my heart at a loss. Something would have to change. I did not know what then, but I knew I needed to go home and this time try and figure myself out.

Much like that Thanksgiving I still felt distant and weary of myself and my future only this time I chose to not close everyone out. I remember the most difficult night of that whole Christmas break was facing the truth to someone in my family. One night while unpacking and settling in for my six weeks at home, I found myself talking to my middle sister. Being only two years apart in age we did have a strong bond and friendship that went deeper than that of just sisters. I confided in her what had happened to me on that night back in November. I remember I made her promise me she would not tell anyone what I had told her that night. I was still uneasy and feeling guilty even though everyone who knew was preaching otherwise and trying to get inside my head. I will never forget my sister and what she looked like when I told her what had happened to me. Her eyes welled with tears, and she just listened to me. I knew she had a thousand thoughts and questions of her own, but she seemed to respect my state of mind and said very little to me. I never realized how much I needed that—someone who knew me as a child to tell me it was not my fault and if nothing else to never lose sight of that one thing, which she knew I did.

I spent the rest of Christmas in silence of the truth. I spoke of my life at college briefly and answered the questions given to me with a short lived smile. By the end of break I found myself returning back to Amherst, but this time with an empty car and the company of a dear friend beside me. She and I drove three hours as I unraveled the truth and began talking to her. I spoke of my night back in November and how I could no longer recognize myself.

When we got to campus, our conversation stopped as we began to work. Within about four hours we were back on the road heading towards the Cape. I had officially dropped out of school. As I drove off that evening I felt a wave of discomfort build in my stomach. I was defeated and now heading home to face something I had yet to face…my reality.

Everything I had worked so hard for was quickly stripped away from me. I gave up my life, my friends, an education, and full athletic scholarship for the following four years. I had left an even larger part of my spirit alive on that field hockey field, but knowing it still lived there made it easier to never let go. I returned home only to face my shame and weakness. I hid myself in fear of what others may see or think. But truthfully that was all wrong, it wasn't until later I realized I was only hiding from those who only wanted to support and protect me. I suppose looking back it is easier to see, but at the time I trusted no one, not even those who loved me. I hid my truth from everyone, as well as the reason why I was behaving in such a manner. I feared them knowing about that night and telling me it was my fault or that I deserved it, so instead I ran away.

Beyond those shadowed memories I chose to do what I wanted, ignore the truth through a drunken stupor, but it only seemed to enhance my problems. There were countless nights I found myself incapable of getting drunk only to get angry until I eventually drank myself sober. Ironically enough, this became the biggest game of my life, and I had been defeated. I ran only because of the pain and terror that raced in my mind. But the faster and further I ran the stronger the nightmare became waking me day and night. Continuing to use alcohol as my medicine I found my only true escape when I was no longer in my own mind. The sense of having no control somehow gave me the impression that I had all the control in the world. I saw myself slipping and quickly. My friends turned me away in fear of my behavior. My reflection began to mirror that of a stranger, and I could only shutter in disgust at my own appearance. My own identity had become a mystery. I became incapable and unable to unravel my past, and I was haunted by one simple question with no answer; Why?

Recovering from that type of an incident may be an actual physical impossibility. Though people have a tendency to say time will heal all, I have come to realize that is not always the case. With this theory we sit and let time pass us by in hopes that with this we are healing when in actuality we are not. What I have found to be the key factor for anyone who does face this is acceptance. No matter how much time does pass you by, if you never truly accept the reality of it, you are never really dealing with anything. Without acceptance we submerge ourselves into a parallel life where we no longer have full control of our minds and actions.

In many ways I am a hypocrite for saying this because I was my own worst enemy. I never accepted what happened to me that night. I tried to dilute my nightmares among waves of alcohol only to intensify every emotion that lived within me. I found myself alone in a cloud of disarray. Luckily after hitting rock bottom on several occasions, I had somewhat of a realization of my life. Yes, maybe I wanted to run in an emotional and physical sense, but until the truth be acknowledged and my experience looked at realistically, I was merely going to run in circles.

Chapter 4

I returned home with the hope to find peace with myself, to discover who I was and who I had become. But the feelings of failure overcame me quickly. If only I could make that night, those four hours, disappear forever. For the first time in my life even the solace of home, Cape Cod, was not easing my pain. I knew I needed to go away and this time somewhere a bit further. So on a whim I found myself once again packing up my belongings. At that time my oldest sister, was the assistant coach and working on her masters at a smaller university in the Midwest. In desperation I called her and arranged to move out that weekend. It may have been a hasty decision, but I knew I needed a change so she graciously took me under her wing.

My goals when I arrived were simple...work and stay as alone as possible. This was an easy transition as my sister ran a very time consuming schedule, which left me on my own for the majority of the day. I got a job bussing tables at a local restaurant. A very family and kids friendly restaurant where I was the only bus person, working about a 55-hour week, but it didn't even phase me. I wanted my mind to be occupied with something other than that night plus I wanted to stay out of any tempting trouble that naturally exists in a college town.

The quaint surroundings served its purpose for me. I had a routine, and I was too busy to do much else except think about that. It is such a wake up call when you spend your days and nights cleaning up after other people. Ground in food in a carpeted dining room with no God damn vacuum. It was practically slave labor. And to top it off I even got to clean the bathrooms at the end of the night, and all for the amazing wage of $5.25 an hour.

Still, even with your hand down a toilet or pushing a broom, it is amazing how much one thought can consume your brain. I wondered if I should take action. I thought a lot about other girls out there who may encounter these men someday and would they do it again or had they done it before? Still I was in no shape to take action. I knew if action was going to be taken I had to be mentally and emotionally more stable. But I was engulfed in that night. Miles away from my past, it still hung thick around me. There were days I felt I would drown in my own mind.

It wasn't until February that my parents drove the fourteen hours out to see me and confessed they knew what had happened to me that November. In all my life I have never felt what I did at that moment. Among tear filled eyes I looked at my parents like a child in trouble, a little girl in need of comfort, in need of her parents. So I made them a promise. I promised to come back home at the end of March and get counseling. I would live at home, work, get back on my feet, and talk to someone who could finally untangle the mess in my head.

As they left that weekend, I felt a weight lifted off my shoulders. I felt I was no longer drowning, no longer hiding from what had happened. I understood then that running away never makes the past disappear. It merely gives you a head start from it catching up to you. Nothing would ever really heal until I let myself accept what had actually happened. Bussing tables was only an escape from reality. But I wasn't ready for an escape yet. So after another six weeks I packed up again and headed back to the Cape to keep the promise I had made with my parents, but not before proudly quitting my job and telling the management staff to please buy a damn vacuum!

Chapter 5

Coming back home was not easy. It was facing the truth. Looking people in the face and letting them fire their judgment at me. I took everything with a small grain of salt the best that I could. When I dropped out, there were inevitably those around me who assumed I only quit school because I could not handle the pressure on the team or I just drank my way to being thrown out of the university. I never took the time to look everyone who thought that in the face and tell them that was not the case at all. I still felt ashamed and embarrassed.

Cape Cod is unfortunately a very small town; so when the athlete randomly drops out of school after only one semester, lets face it, they are going to talk. After all I was the first senior to sign my letter of intent and know where I was going to school so this was the new big gossip around town. Truth is it ate away at me. As much as I wanted to let them talk, I also wanted to shout out to the world what had really happened. But I never did. I kept my family and true friends close. The ones who stood by were the ones who knew the truth and only wanted to help me heal. They knew how to make the pain subside, even if it was just for a moment. Still I felt angry and confused, I had no understanding as to why I had to give up my life for something someone else had done. I kept asking why, why me, why now? But still I never wished my experience upon anyone else.

In some ways I always felt if someone was to go through a traumatic experience I was the best one because I was still determined enough to fight through it. Granted at times I didn't always do this in the healthiest of ways, but still I was surviving even though that was difficult to see some days. When someone steals your innocence and betrays you, you feel as though you've grown a million years older in that very instant, which I did. At eighteen I had given up a life known to set out into something I had never known. I needed to start over with my same values and morals at heart. Only this was easier said than done. Instead I tried so hard to shield the pain but desperately wanting to run.

That April I got a job as a hostess/waitress at a very busy and popular restaurant on the water. It wasn't my favorite job, but it was busy and passed the time quickly. I barely had time to think during my eight-hour shift. I spent the summer continuing old habits, drinking excessively to numb my pain. I was dating a guy much older, so getting into bars underage was much easier than expected. It also helped that he knew basically everyone on the Cape. I knew my heart would not be close to him but he gave me an outlet. He was a true escape from reality. At the time, looking back, I needed him and I thank him for that.

Aside from the occasional two week dating games, I did a good job at staying single while I was unraveling my head. I knew I had no strength to give anyone anything of value so I did what I had to get close, but then run in the other direction before anything could get too serious. I definitely had some commitment issues, but could anyone really blame me for that? Around June I found the same haunting thoughts waking me in the middle of the night. I feared mostly the other girls out there who might experience what I had gone through. So with revenge in sight and my parents by my side, I decided I was ready to do something. I had started the therapy as promised and felt some of my issues becoming clearer. I knew I wanted to proceed forward, and my goal was to make those guys pay for their crime. I wanted to stop at nothing less than jail time. I wouldn't be happy unless I knew they were behind bars and not at risk of hurting some other innocent victim. I had already been hurt, but I wanted to prevent and help anyone else out there. I wanted to be a voice. I wanted just one person to learn something from my story. So my mother and I drove back up to the college town to speak with the campus police and file my case.

Just being back on the campus gave me an unsettling feeling, and it was then I knew I would never have been able to stay there and finish my academics. The detective was a very strong young woman who wanted to help me in achieving what I set out for. The most difficult thing she made me do was tell my story. As I began, it wasn't long before she stopped me. She was sincere and gentle but told me that when she said "tell" she meant tell. That meant in very explicit detail. After I realized what she was looking for, I began to start talking all over again. I made several trips with my mom, speaking with her, and giving my story. Soon after she was ready for me to officially file my report. Again she sat me in front of a blank computer screen and told me to start typing. I will never forget her words telling me to be as explicit as possible and if it sounded embarrassing, then it probably should be written.

After questioning friends, teammates, and the four boys, we were ready to go forward. My detective said the story was black and white and this case was going to go forward, meaning she thought I would be taking them to court in front of a judge and jury. All the police reports had been filed and it was clear as day the boys were guilty. I was happy for the first time in a while. I was going to have my revenge and my voice would be heard. The last step before the case could go forward was to have the district attorney review the case and make the final decision if we were to go to trial or not.

That car ride with my mother that day seemed forever. I just wanted to get there and get this all to go forward. I was so confident they would have to pay for their actions. Much to my mom, the detective, and my surprise, the district attorney denied the case and refused to go forward. I was shocked; it felt like someone had taken the air right out of my lungs and stuck a knife directly through my heart. How could she not understand what everyone else could see so clearly? Something needed to be done and she refused. Coming from another woman I was most surprised. All I kept thinking was how many people try to reinforce women reporting if they had been raped because too many cases, especially at colleges, go unreported to the police. The DA said she was afraid I would not be mentally prepared to go through four separate trials, one for each of the boys. I never understood how my emotional state could determine whether this was right or wrong. I knew deep in my heart I was ready to do this. I tried pleading with her that had this been right after the incident I probably was not ready but now with the support of my family, friends and counseling, I did truly feel ready to take action. My final words to her that dreary June day were "Fuck off." I had no energy to say anything else. That was that and what was done was done, and I had no say otherwise. Somehow those words I left on were all I could seem to get out at that moment.

The drive home was grueling, and I could not help feeling the DA had made me feel even guiltier for what had happened. About a month or so later I received a letter in the mail from that same DA. She told me she often thought about me and wanted me to call the college where one of the boys went and tell them they had a sex offender enrolled in their school and on their campus. How could that be? Here she was admitting these guys were sex offenders but afraid to let me do something. I knew that letter was simply her guilty conscience eating her away inside, and it was simply her attempt to put me and my face out of her mind. To this day I still hope she remembers my case and my final words to her. I hope my face and my tears from that day wake her up every night.

Like many Cape Cod restaurants the one I worked at closed for the season in late October, leaving me unemployed once again. Not long after, I was hired as a duty-aide at my former middle school. It was a temporary move where I only worked part time till something else came along. I went to work every day from 9 to 2. It was so strange to be back in the halls I grew up in. Only now I was so much older with so much of life behind me and so much sadness lived in my soul. I found myself feeling envious of the children. I wanted to go back and be in that life again. However, I enjoyed having the innocence of so many children around me. They gave me a different way of looking at things.

It always amazes me how a child sees the world. For me the children's eyes became my eyes into a new future. They saw me for only what they wanted to see. There was no judgment or ridicule. I was a hero in their eyes just because I was taking time to be with them and listen to what they had to say. In all my life I never needed anything more than that. I never knew the power of the child's mind and heart until then. They had inspired me. Standing on the playground one day, I looked around me. There among the children I felt something I had never felt before. I felt inspired.

I realized in a way I could go back. Maybe not back to the sixth grade, but I could go back to school. I could have a second chance if I really wanted it. That was the key though, I knew I needed to want to go back and only I could really decide that. It was the innocence among those children that inspired my next move to get a second job, only this one paid nothing.

Chapter 6

While occupying my morning hours at the middle school, my afternoons revolved around the new gym I joined...my second job. I had been out of school for only a year until the drive to go back hit me hard. I wanted the chance to play field hockey again. I wanted a chance to gain a part of my life back, a part of myself I missed and I knew I could only achieve this on the field. I had to go back to what I knew. I had to be like those children, I had to regain my innocence and go back to what I knew best. I wanted to play. I know I cannot ever remember the names of all those kids, but I do know I will never forget any of them and the things they taught me and the things I learned from them. Little did they know their "teacher" had learned more from them than they could have ever learned from me.

I had a lot of things to do when I made the decision to get back into the game. I had nine months to contact coaches and get myself back into shape. Getting into shape would be the easy part, but for the first time I had to do my own networking with the coaches. It wasn't like before when the coaches came to me, this time I had to go to them.

Unfortunately when I dropped out, many of the coaches in the "coaching circle" had heard the same rumors that many others had heard. So much to my dismay, the answer on the other end was not always received with enthusiasm. How could this be? I had done nothing wrong and now even coaches were judging me, only they were judging me for what they knew nothing about. To them I was nothing but a washed up "has been" who was out of the game for a year. Still I held my hope in my hands and forged on. Luckily with the help of my oldest sister I gained some interest from the school she had been coaching at in the Midwest. Her graduate position would be over in May and I could start that August so the timing would be perfect. When she graduated from grad school in May, I accompanied my parents on the eighteen-hour car ride to meet the coach and finalize some plans.

Fortunately I was headed back to a familiar ground, but a campus of unfamiliar faces. The head coach was excited to have me join her upcoming team but informed me that I needed to attend summer school on the Cape over the next few months to be eligible to play in the fall season. So I returned home to finish her orders. Because of my low GPA at my one semester of school, I needed to get nothing under a B+ in order to be accepted at the new school.

That was a busy summer for my family. After Ann's graduation in May from grad school, we were preoccupied with her wedding which was over fourth of July weekend. She was marrying a man she had met at college and we all had known for many years. I was excited to gain a brother in the family. With so much going on, however, I needed to continue to focus on my goals with school and getting into shape.

I had a strict physical training program to be up to Division I capacity, but I was not afraid of the challenge at hand. So I ran, literally. For the first time in awhile I was running with a goal in sight. With each painful step I was closer and closer to the field. I could see the competition and taste the revenge. After the rape I knew one way to gain my revenge was to go back and get my second chance at field hockey. Something they had taken so suddenly from my life was now so close. I truly believed that stepping foot back on a field somewhere would only reinforce my strength and determination towards overcoming my past.

Some people will say when a person is raped they go through several stages of recovery. Some of them being guilt, depression, anger, destruction, revenge, solitude and promiscuity. I can proudly say I went through each one of these. But revenge came in several forms. Playing field hockey was the least harmful and most sane of my options. Anyway, I finished my courses at summer school by August 8th and waited anxiously to see my grades before packing the car and getting my hopes up. Much to everyone's surprise I finished with an A and an A-. So that was it. I was on my way back to college and gaining a part of my life back.

I had arranged to live off-campus in my sister's house, which she had moved out of, with her two old roommates. I knew coming into a new school where I knew nobody and being a 20-year-old freshman was going to be hard. So I wanted nothing to do with the dorm lifestyle. So once again I moved into my new "home" and waved goodbye to my parents. Again, I felt that sinking feeling in my stomach, but this time I had a different determination, different goals, and more of life behind me. I had learned my hard lessons and was confident not to make the same mistakes again.

As my parent's car faded into the distance, I went back inside the house and cried. There, on the table next to the bed, was a small book entitled, *I Believe in You*. On the inside cover it read:

> This is a new beginning for you. You are a much stronger person for all you have been through. Remember all of our life's experiences, good and bad, always travel with us throughout our entire lives. We can't leave the good times or the bad times behind. They are all part of the person we become. You have learned from both the good and the bad. You are ready now to go out again and pursue your dreams. I love you and believe in you. You are my very special baby!

Love and God Bless, Mom, xxoo.

I wiped my eyes dry, swallowed hard, and headed for the door. It was time for my first practice. As I neared the field, I smiled to myself thinking about what my mom had said and what the book was about. My mother always had a way of letting me know she never gave up on me and always believed in me. I still keep that book in my bedroom, and on days when I feel lost or sad, I look at it and remember that day she left it for me. It will always be a reminder of that day and how I fought so hard to get myself back to school after all that had happened.

I was so thankful to have this second chance that I knew I worked so hard for. I got to practice early and many days stayed late to work on my skills. I had been on the "sidelines" so-to-speak for a year and half so I felt I had a lot of time to make up. I did feel I had an unfair advantage over my teammates though, and that advantage was appreciation. I had already experienced the real world when I dropped out once, so I was gracious every minute to have such an amazing comeback to something I loved so much. I became the prime example of someone who had hit rock bottom only to go up again. I was finally back in a college atmosphere with a full scholarship to play a game I truly loved. I could not believe how far I had come.

I did focus most of my energy on the field, but this time I managed to do at least what I needed in the classroom to stay eligible. The whole college transition was a little harder this time around. For starters I was much further away from home and I knew nobody. Also I was a transfer student. I was academically a freshman, on the field I was a sophomore, but my age put me at a junior grade level. So I had no real group to step into. Plus many of the girls only knew me as their assistants younger sister so I wanted to prove myself to them. It didn't take long for me to find my area and gain my respect from the others on the field. I had met a whole new group of friends who wanted to know me and where I had come from. They respected my background and playing for such a highly skilled and well known team prior to that. In return I opened myself slowly to them. With time I had found a new place to call home and new people who I loved like family.

Just as I began to find myself in this small town the unexpected happened yet again. At a very early morning practice I felt a pain in my leg I had never experienced before. At the end of practice and behind closed doors the pain brought me to tears. I returned to the afternoon practice earlier than the team to find my trainer awaiting my arrival. She knew something was wrong. I was scheduled for an MRI that afternoon. Unfortunately what I had hoped to be a simple muscle pull was something worse.

The MRI revealed I had two bulging discs in my lower back causing nerve pain down my leg. The diagnosis left me on the sidelines for the first six weeks of the season. I was devastated. I had never had a back problem or any serious injury before, and I felt my dreams just dissipate before my eyes. I was used to always playing through any pain, but this time the injury was out of my hands. I remember sitting in my room and just crying. It was the hardest I had cried in a long time. I was so far from home with not a familiar shoulder to lean on. I had all my teammates support, but I just wanted a familiar face in that moment, I wanted my family. It was days before our first game and I had to watch from a familiar seat, the sidelines. It was the most I had ever missed my family. With the support of my teammates and the drive in my heart, I was determined to go through the rigorous six weeks of physical therapy, combined with a swimming workout, after the regular practices that I would watch from afar.

As soon as I met Mike, the physical therapist, I felt at ease. He was positive and determined to help me recover. He was my sanity those six weeks. I would see him three or four times a week and he worked me hard. He knew how devastated I was so he did all in his power to help me get back on that field. If nothing else, he became a great friend to me at that time and helped me emotionally as well as mentally. I felt like I had found a different kind of therapist. I don't know if it was the injury, the timing or just the void of my family that allowed me to open myself to him, but I know whatever it was I was thankful for him. We had a great bond; he used to call me his little sister and I really felt like it. We would fight, argue, and laugh just like family. It was the perfect medicine that kept me thinking I would make it through this tough time in my life.

Luckily the six weeks of therapy, pain medicines, and two epidurals relieved most of the nerve pain allowing me to finally get on the field for half a game. It was one step at a time from that moment on. My first practice back was intimidating. Not only was I hesitant to re-injure myself, but I was now six weeks down on my running workouts. I knew I was a step behind in everything. My physical shape was no longer intact with my mental strength. I knew my potential and performance on the field was being held back from my injury. It was as though mentally I was so far ahead of my physical ability. When I sat with my coaches, I would tell them in my head I am getting the ball but on the field my body was just not there. It is a frustrating feeling knowing what you can do but not being able to actually do it. Much to everyone's surprise I did finish out that season, but when the curtain fell on that final game, the curtain also fell on my collegiate career as that game would be my final reign on any field.

Chapter 7

As Thanksgiving break came closer, I noticed my pain coming back even worse. I went back for my second MRI which revealed a ruptured disc in my lower back. I was tentatively scheduled for a routine discectomy the Monday after Thanksgiving break. When I went home for the holiday, I got a second opinion from a doctor at home. He also agreed a routine surgery would be the most beneficial. So after the break I went back to Ohio to have my surgery that Monday morning. I felt confident seeing as though the doctor in Ohio had operated on several other athletes at the school and was giving me a 99.9% recovery rate. I even had a friend who played football that I met in physical therapy that had the same surgery the previous year and was now back on the field. The doctor assured me that, with the proper physical therapy following the surgery, I would have a full recovery and be playing field hockey again the next year.

Willingly I agreed to the procedure and found myself under the knife the Monday following Thanksgiving break. This type of surgery is done very frequently and usually has very positive results; unfortunately this would not be the case for me. I spent one night at the hospital and returned back to school the next day. I was advised to take the rest of the week off from class and stay in bed at all cost, which is what I did. My oldest sister actually came out to stay with me. It was so nice to have a family member there with me. We watched movies, hung out, and chatted for hours. My mom and dad could not come out because at the same time my middle sister was having health problems of her own.

Unlike what was supposed to be happening after the surgery, my body seemed to disagree with the procedure. I never felt the instant relief everyone had talked to me about. Typically, when you have this type of surgery, as soon as the disc material is released from the nerve, the pain should subside. The only pain you should feel afterwards is from the incision. I never felt that relief. My pain would subside for a couple of days and then intensify for a couple of days. It became a vicious cycle that was apparent as clockwork. I had never had any back problems so I simply thought this to be normal. I finished out the semester with the same pain and returned home three weeks later for Christmas break. For most students Christmas break is about catching up with old friends and family and just being able to relax and enjoy the holidays. Mine wasn't exactly like that.

Elizabeth's health issues had come to a head when her doctors told us she was to have brain surgery. She had been having up to twenty seizures a day for the past three years or so. They only lasted ten to fifteen seconds or so, and she never really knew how to tell anyone about what she was experiencing so she did her best to hide it from us. The first time I saw her have a seizure it just looked as if she was somewhere completely else, somewhere distant, and then that was it. So naturally they were somewhat easy for her to hide for such a long time. After having a seizure in front of my parents at the dinner table one night, she was brought to the emergency room. It was later that they realized she had a malformation of blood vessels, which had caused a bleed in her brain. It had all happened so suddenly, and she needed to have surgery to prevent any further complications.

She was scheduled for brain surgery in Boston on January 7, 2000, just five days before I was to return to school. It was an unusual Christmas that year. My sisters and I are all very close so to watch any one of us have to go through such an intense surgery was difficult for everyone to cope with. Meanwhile, my back was getting worse, but I didn't want to make any matters worse at home. So, instead, I tried as hard as I could to just ignore the pain. My concern was now primarily with my sister.

We had all planned to be in Disney World for the millennium, it was something my mother had planned about eight years prior. My whole family are Disney fanatics, and we went practically every year so naturally my mom had planned to celebrate the year 2000 in our favorite place. The doctors insisted we still go on the trip in hopes that it might be a good distraction for everyone at that time. So we did. The truth was you could tell we were all preoccupied about Elizabeth's surgery. But with faith in our hearts, my entire family celebrated 2000 down in the "Happiest Place on Earth." It was a great trip. Even with everything ahead of us, we still all had fun just being together. But after many late nights and a lot of fun, we all headed back north to face a bigger reality.

On the morning of January 7th my whole family awaited restlessly in the hospital for my sisters surgery to be completed. It was going to be a six hour procedure. At six in the morning I watched her walk down the hall as the door closed slowly behind her. It is such a helpless feeling watching someone you love walk into something you have no control over. To this day I will never fully understand the fear that must have lived in my sister's mind that morning as she said goodbye to all of us or the uncertainty in all of us as she faded out of sight. It was the longest six hours of my life. You could sense the fear and anxiety in the air. We did only what we could do, wait. Around one o'clock we finally got word that the surgery had been a success and we could visit with her in a few hours. You could actually feel the relief lift over that waiting room as we knew she was going to be fine. God had been with us.

The hardest part for me was having to see my sister and then get on a plane to head back out to school for my spring semester. She was still in intensive care when I said goodbye to her. I suppose nobody really could have prepared me for that goodbye. How could I even think about school, classes or anything else? I wanted so badly to just be with my family. It is amazing how such difficult situations make a person realize how alone they can be. For me returning back to school left me with such an alone feeling in my heart. But somehow when we least expect it, we find some ounce of strength that carries us forward in life. It carried me that day, onto that plane, and back out to school.

Chapter 8

Due to the excess stress surrounding my sister's surgery, I had failed to tell my parents, or anybody for that matter, how I had been feeling and the pain I was enduring. I failed to tell them that one entire leg was completely numb now with no feeling in it. The pain became unbearable. It was only two weeks later that I reached my point where my strength no longer existed. A final trip to the doctors and another MRI revealed another ruptured disc in my back.

With my sister still home on bed rest, my mom insisted I come home for the second surgery. She was too afraid of being far from my side. Plus with each back surgery you have, the longer the recovery can take. The doctors felt emergency surgery would be essential before I lost total feeling in my leg forever. So without any further questions or hesitation, I packed up my belongings, yet again, and returned home. I flew in on a Saturday and had my surgery that Monday night. The doctor thought the procedure would only take a maximum of an hour. At eight o'clock or so, I went into the operating room and three and a half hours later I came out. To the surgeons surprise, when I was opened up he found not only a disc particle but also a hemorrhagic cyst that had formed on the spinal cord.

The doctors concluded that in my first surgery something had been nicked causing a blood pocket the size of a quarter to fill with fluid. When the fluid would fill completely, it would cause the most amount of pain due to its size, then it would burst and the fluid would drain down my leg, which would relieve most of the leg pain at the same time. This finally revealed the mysterious clockwork cycle of pain that I had been experiencing for the past couple of months. Both the original doctor and my new surgeon at home had never seen anything like this before. Due to the excess strain on the back in the same location, I was put on strict bed rest for eight to ten weeks.

Basically it meant as little physical activity as possible reassuring the recovery and avoiding any further damage. I spent those weeks in a mild state of depression. You cannot avoid the weird mental state your mind goes through when you are confined to a bed for such a long time. You actually feel insane. I spent my time like an infant with my days and nights confused. I would sleep for most of the day and then stay up all night. Sometimes today when I feel stressed from life, I look back at that time in my life when I could do nothing. It is so ironic, when you have no time in the world you want to be able to just sit and do nothing, then suddenly you are granted all the time in the world and you sadly realize how little you have to do. I spent the majority of my time that spring writing. It was my only release of all that was living in my head.

Following the doctors orders, I reached a full recovery by about April with no residual leg pain. With time I only continued to feel better. I started a therapy program on my own, walking. It was slow at first but in a couple of months

I was walking three to four miles a day with ease. It was a slow transition from running to walking, but I knew any activity would have to be better than nothing at all, and it was. I had never realized the strain a bad back can have on one's life. I had known others who had problems, my mom for starters, but I never comprehended her pain until I experienced it myself. So I kept positive and knew the slow process would only pay off in the end. To this day I will always have a new found understanding and respect for anyone who experiences back pain. It truly is debilitating.

That spring I had thought a lot about going back to school for summer school. It was a great way to make up the classes I had to drop out of in a short time frame. So I had arranged to go back in May under strict guidelines from my doctor. The session was only six weeks, and I was able to move right back into the house I had been in. I was about four months out of surgery and starting to feel like myself again. I was looking forward to spending summer school with some friends who were out there and living back in my old house again. So in May I packed up some things and headed back to familiar territory. I was taking two classes and continuing my walking regime on a daily basis.

Those six weeks were the best time of my college career. A lot of the athletes stay for summer school so I had most of my friends out there with me. Plus the population of students is so much smaller and the nightlife is actually better. It was my kind of school, six weeks and class was over. I turned twenty-one on June 11 of that summer. With all my friends there to help me celebrate, it was a night to not be forgotten. Even though it was not my first drink, there is still something unexplainable about your first legal drink; of course, at that point in the night, I remembered only moments of what it felt like. Like most twenty-first birthdays, you actually live them through the stories you here about the next day from those that were there in a more sober state. Still from what I remember it was a great time.

A few of the other girls on the field hockey team were around so occasionally we would get together and go play down at the turf. It was the first time I had gotten to just play in so long. I never thought I would be back out there, but I did it. I felt so good. I was healthy, I was walking, and even running a bit when I could. I could feel my passion burning inside and I knew I wanted to play again. I wanted to have another chance. There seemed to be a light at the end of my tunnel. I felt so alive just being able to play at all. I had come so far and was ready to keep going. I felt proud knowing I had come back to school despite my back and my history at my first college. Regardless if I ever actually played field hockey competitively or not was now not as much of a concern. I was in a strange place, making friends, feeling at home, and focusing on one last goal I had in sight...graduating. It was still far in the distance but at the same time at least it was there. For the first time my academics took precedence over athletics. I knew, if nothing else, I was going to finish my commitment at school.

Chapter 9

I went back to the Cape after summer school that year to see my family and friends and make some money. My parents owned a gift shop for twenty-five years so I went there to work and spend time with my mom. Along with that I was still continuing my walking and now swimming for my own therapy. Each day I was feeling better and stronger. Those walks became my own kind of therapy. My sanity. For an hour or so I would reflect on my life, where I had been, and the things I had gone through. I started mentally writing my life in my head. I imagined so many endings in sight.

I do that a lot, I play things in my head and try and see the ending before it actually happens. Maybe I am just still a kid daydreaming at heart or maybe that was just the writer that exists deep inside me asleep and destined to be awoken. With each step I would take, I was releasing anger from my past and breathing in my new life. I felt I was energizing my mind and soul in a different kind of way. Something that could not have been done by "normal" therapy where you sit in front of someone who just writes down each word you say. But it was paying off in other ways too, I was doing so well, in fact, that my doctor even cleared me to play field hockey again if I wanted to try for the fall season. I knew then that I had an even greater light at the end my tunnel, another chance to compete and play what I loved more than anything else. Unfortunately, like some things, it was too good to be true.

About a week before I was to return to school, I skipped my morning walk to accompany my mother to breakfast instead. It was an early, rainy day, so I was glad to not be fighting the weather outside. The streets were busy as usual with all kinds of people on their way out and about. About five miles from our house I felt a loud crash behind us then followed by another. Two vehicles had struck us from behind. I can remember looking at my mother with sadness in my eyes. All I could manage to say to her at that moment was, "My back." I felt the pain immediately.

My mom and I went to the hospital to have x-rays, and then I went to see my doctor who had performed my back surgery. The accident had jolted my back but I didn't want to even think about it. I knew then that the accident vanished my hopes of ever playing field hockey again. That faint glimmer of hope was now indefinitely gone forever. Still I set my heart on returning to school. My doctor was afraid to let me leave and advised me to stay for the semester to avoid any damage that may have already been done, but I refused. I was too tired of sitting at home, and I wanted to be back at school. I was determined to not miss another full semester of school.

So I packed the car and headed back to school. As I drove away, I knew deep down that there was a good chance I would be returning home sooner than later. I kept trying to tell myself I was fine and the pain was not there, but inside

I could not deny what I felt. It was a similar pain from before and a pain I knew all too well and was all too familiar with.

This was my first time at school not having field hockey to keep me grounded. Also, I had moved into the dorms with two of my friends. I had more free time than I had ever imagined. All my friends were still athletes who had busy schedules and traveled a lot. On most weekends my roommates were traveling or busy with practice and home games. I spent more time writing only this time I was writing to release my anger. I hated where I was. I hated that I got into that car that morning. I didn't know what to do with my time or myself. Many days I would sit alone, isolated, and just sad. I wanted to go back in time. I found myself reliving many moments in my life especially the rape and my life back then. But somehow just when things seem down they can have a way of turning around when you least expect it and they did. His name was John.

Chapter 10

Though I had dated other guys during my time at school I was still reluctant and hesitant to really get close to anyone. After my experience at my first college I wanted nothing from anyone of the opposite sex. I felt too afraid, and I knew I had no trust to offer in a relationship. I had made a routine of dating people just long enough and then leaving before I had to get too serious about it. Many rape victims experience this train of thought. We find comfort in hurting the opposite sex because somehow it makes us feel powerful. I went through this process for a long time and initially my intentions were going to be the same with John, but somehow that didn't work.

Normally my brain could simply tell myself what to do as well as how and when to walk away from someone. I admit it there was some sick and twisted enjoyment to hurting other people. I wanted them to feel the pain I was feeling just for a second. With John the harder I tried to pull away from him the more I was pulled toward him. It was the first time in my life I could not let my brain overpower my heart. It was a force I could not reckon with.

I had that instant connection with him. The one that catches you so off guard you cannot even seem to explain it or understand it, so you don't, you just take things as they come and let fate happen. But nothing is ever that easy. The more I saw of John, the more he intrigued me. He was a football player for starters. I mean how could I ever date a football player? But more importantly he had an ex-girlfriend of three years. An ex-girlfriend, whom he informed me shortly after we had met, that he was getting back together with. I felt crushed for the first time in awhile about a guy. He had been such a great distraction for me and from field hockey and now I felt I would lose that for sure. But his three-year history with his ex in my eyes was no competition for the month we had only known each other. So I did what I could do to simply forget about him, only that proved hard for both of us to do. Still I hated the idea of being the third wheel.

John never went away regardless of his girlfriend; in fact he called me more and wanted to see me more than ever. I knew he wanted to take a chance, but at the same time he was too scared of me. Too scared to take a chance with someone who had no ability to trust. I was so caught up in this mystery of him, this person who tested my inhibitions. Normally I would not have been so attached, why was this so different? I couldn't answer my own questions and became my own worst enemy in the situation. Instead of taking a chance myself I hid from him. I was afraid to let him know me, and I was afraid to let him hurt me. Each time I let him get close I ran before he could ever really know me. I played these games for quite awhile and let him be with his girlfriend. In the mean time, I continued to date other people solely to make him jealous. I admit maybe it wasn't the most mature way to handle my real feelings but it worked at the time, although, I am not advising anyone out there to do it.

If only I had been honest with him and how I felt at first, he may have taken a chance with me. But instead I shielded myself and pretended not to care. I will never know how that affected us in the end, and I cannot beat myself up about it. The longer we kept from one another the more consumed we were with each another. It became months upon months of these constant games and we were both addicted to it, but more honestly we were addicted to one another. I finally was feeling a love I had not known in such a long time. But still I had a mask on that I could not bear to remove for him. I couldn't reveal it to anyone. I wanted John to just see me as a carefree girl who wanted nothing to do with a relationship. Only that could not have been further from the truth. What I was feeling was just something I just had not let myself feel in such a long time. Fortunately for myself he could read me like a book.

Chapter 11

With my thoughts completely consumed by John, I had little time for much else other than to figure out a way to tell him how I felt and what I wanted. It is such a shame what traumatic experiences do to the human mind. It is the things they never tell you about that become the hardest to cope with. For me it always appeared in relationships. I felt insecure, inferior, and ashamed. I honestly thought a person like John could never really love someone like myself because of all the excess baggage I carried with me. I mean, when I entered a relationship, I came with about sixteen bags of emotional damage behind me. So each time I would feel I could get close to him, I would run even faster in the opposite direction, sixteen bags and all. Christmas break could not have come at a better time that year. I knew I needed some time to clear my head of him and this whole situation. Like before I needed to be around my comfortable environment to really get a clearer picture of things. I needed to escape from those surroundings and just not think for a while. However, from miles away, the heart only grows deeper and I only thought about John more with each day. It was then I realized my heart had grown weak and needed to be honest.

While at home I also returned to see my doctor. Another MRI revealed a piece of disc was encased in scar tissue and muscle and was pressing on the nerve. It would only be a matter of time before it would have to be removed with a third surgery. It's funny, when I was at school, I seemed less distracted by my pain because I had this larger vice in my life that occupied my brain. Against the doctors will, I returned back to school for the spring in the hopes of battling my feelings and facing my truth. I put my health aside and wanted to face my fears head on. I was prepared to finally reveal the mask which hid my identity and open myself to this man I had been so consumed by.

In a lot of ways I used John as a way to hide from the pain that existed in my body. He became my only positive at school and my only true reason for returning that semester only he did not know it. My intentions of letting us grow apart never happened, as I only grew closer towards him. So with my nerves on fire, I called him and insisted that we talk. I remember sitting in his car behind the football stadium, my hands were cold and my heart paced faster than it had ever known. I finally confessed to him what had happened to me years before and how I really cared for him. I hid nothing and let my guard down completely to another man for the first time since the rape. I wanted to end the games and be honest; I wanted to love again. It was that night I sensed his feelings back towards me, I felt invincible. But still fate had another test in store for me and for us.

It was not long after that night that John told me he wanted to take a chance with me and only me. He had ended his relationship, (or so I thought). I felt my honesty had paid off, and I was finally awarded with an opportunity with someone I adored. The only thing that now stood in my way was the numbing pain in my leg that I had known so many times before. It was the first time I had to pay attention to it and could no longer ignore its severity. With little strength to even walk, I knew I had to handle my health. Sure enough, just a week later, I had to return home for my third back surgery. Just like that I said farewell to John with our relationship ending even quicker than it had begun. I had hopes of returning that May, but I knew it was too soon to tell.

The night before I left was John's birthday. I felt certain there was only one gift I could give him. It was something I had written for him months before but was always too afraid to let him read. It was everything I had wanted to say but had never had the chance to say to him. It was also the first thing I had written that wasn't fueled by anger, it was merely my heart speaking out loud. So I left it with him, rolled up in my cheap silver crown ring that I had always worn. I hoped he would feel my heart and voice simply through my words. I barely had the strength to say goodbye so in a way I didn't, instead I just said, "goodnight."

Goodnight

Sometimes at night when darkness falls
My mind slowly melts by the sound of your calls.
It's like a blade that so sharply wounds my skin
And sets my heart afire from a deepness within.

It's unexplainable to one's own naked eye
But uncontrollably certain as it makes me cry.

Amongst a shadowed array of untold secrets
I must tell you now I have no regrets.

As if some dream created has become my own fate
One can only wonder what together we may create.
Some drunken display of a misguided mind
And the eager voices we await to scare blind.

But somehow since this reality has so quietly spoken,
Something inside has suddenly awoken;
Is this merely a night left six days to speak,
Lost beyond time then instantly left weak.?

I am left questioned to what you really do see
As my heart awaits hoping not to flee.
So let it be heard these words that I say
But know now and always tomorrow brings a new day.

Upon the sunrise that so softly calms my breath
I am involved now but this shall not be my death.
My soul may dance lavishly in plain sight
In search of you as this may be our last night.

You may be silent as I think innocently aloud
But somehow these words speak sweetly and proud.
So maybe I must decide from here where to fly
Away from my truth and let my feelings die.

So patiently I remain and allow your soul to be free
To rest assured just this once the story ends with me.

With that said I was quickly on a plane flying away from
who I wanted and where I wanted to be. The only thought
that helped to ease my pain was my mom's infamous

words, "If it's meant to be, it will be." I was starting to hate those words. It was as though nothing I wanted was meant to be but I tried desperately to take my faith with me on that plane. I had to also leave a small part of my faith behind as I took care of the larger problem at hand. Still, in addition to John, I was already missing my friends. Living on campus really allowed me to become even closer to all of them. They all became like a big family to me. Living only doors apart from each other these things just happen. I was sad knowing I wasn't going to have them when I got home.

Still my pain ran deepest with my thoughts of John and it never ceased to bring me to tears. I wondered if I would ever see him again and if we would ever really get a chance to be together. That was all I ever really wanted. I just wanted a chance to be with him and only him. I wanted him to know me for all my flaws, and in return, I wanted him to let go of his past to just be with me. I hadn't been home longer than two hours before I was greeted by his voice on the phone. He had called to thank me for the gift I had left for him. I was only sorry I could not have been there with him, but still I was just so happy to hear his voice. It was the only remedy for the grief that existed deep in my chest. He gave me the ability to concentrate on my back and getting better. It was the first time I hated the idea of being home. I simply wanted to be with him, but I knew I had to force myself to think only about my health at that moment in time if I ever wanted the chance to return to school that May.

Being my third surgery there was another decision to be made. It is routine with back injuries that with a third surgery a spinal fusion should be done. This usually requires a minimum of a sixteen-week recovery and in some instances a loss of mobility when the procedure is complete. I had several opinions with doctors who thought this was the best avenue for me. I had my age on my side so they thought I would recover with more ease. However, I was hesitant about anything that could possibly limit my mobility in any way. I knew this procedure was not right for me at this point in my life.

Fortunately, the doctor who did my second surgery agreed to try another discectomy to remove the disc material. The surgery had about a less than 30% chance of even working and most likely would only last for about one to two years. Still I wanted to take my chances. It was March of that spring when I had my third and final back surgery. I was put on bed rest once again and spent my weeks in bed writing. It was all too familiar, however, this time my writing was less angry, all my feelings in my head for John began to pour onto paper. It felt so good to just talk without anyone criticizing. Mainly my thoughts were driven by my heart, which had been left so open out at school.

In between my writing I had something else occupying my time, talking to John, we started talking more than ever. Conversations would last hours into the early morning and we never sat with silence. We developed something we really had needed, a friendship. He became my shoulder to cry on when things were difficult at home, and I became a shoulder for him when he needed my help and support. It was amazing how much we opened ourselves to one another.

In late April my Mom, Ann and I took a last minute trip to Antigua in the Caribbean. It was what we all needed. I was sorry my other sister could not have been there with us. But we still managed to enjoy the warm weather, good food, and relaxing atmosphere. One early morning as I sat outside our beach hut in the sun, I looked out onto the horizon and felt a calm feeling overcome my body. I took in the air and smiled. For once I knew exactly what I wanted in my life. When the trip ended and we returned home, my mom asked me if I wanted to transfer to a school back in Massachusetts in case I needed to come home again. I understood her concern but simply told her I had to go back to the Midwest.

I had left some things in my life unfinished, and I needed to return back so I would never have any regrets. I told my mother I needed to give my heart a chance and with that I packed again and left for my second year of summer school. I was getting pretty accustomed to doing my school year in just the fall and summer, as I had never finished a spring semester in all my years of college. My entire plane ride was occupied with the thoughts of seeing John again. It had been three months without the sight of him, and I just wanted to be near him. It was the first time I was able to leave home without tears and with a feeling of excitement in my mind. I had learned so much from my time away from him, and I wanted to give us a chance once and for all. I was ready to let the past fade and face my fears once and for all. That summer I lived with my good friend Liza in a great apartment complex. It was the place where most kids lived for summer school so we had plenty of people around that we knew.

The moment I saw John I felt a nervous anxious feeling. My heart paced in anguish. It had been so long and I had so much to say to him. We spent the summer like a couple, only we weren't. John still had his girlfriend, which I knew, and still hated. I loved his friendship, but I was ready for something more. I wanted us to be together, and I did not want to just be the other girl. So I made many attempts to just walk away from him regardless of our friendship and my desire for him. However, I could never seem to just walk away from it. I always saw other girls in these situations and I wondered why they just couldn't walk away and now here I was, my own worst critic, my very own hypocrite. The six weeks faded fast and once again I left to come back home and work with my mom. I needed to make some money as I was determined to finish a full school year for the first time in my life that fall. Most of all I wanted and needed to walk away with my heart held high. I left John with an ultimatum...either just me or nothing at all. I didn't even want his friendship if he couldn't start making decisions. It was something I should have done long before. He was going to have another six weeks without me there and I prayed to let his heart speak the truth for him, which apparently it did.

By that fall, just six weeks later, I got what I had wished for, a relationship with John. That fall of 2001 I not only returned to school but I returned into the arms of love. This was it; there were no more surgeries, no more ex-girlfriends, and no more dating. I wanted to be with him, and I finally had the chance to do that.

Chapter 12

May 2001 school year was definitely my favorite year of all. I moved back on campus to a single room but shared a suite with one of my best friends, Mary. John lived down the street but we spent all of our time together. It was his senior year with football, which kept him busy, but we managed to spend every other minute we had together. We had both decided to keep our relationship low key at first with both his family and mine because we did not want too much pressure on us. Plus John only lived forty-five minutes away, and I did not want the pressure of meeting his family right away. I was still easing into the whole idea of a relationship. Eventually that did change but for the time we just enjoyed being together.

Things at home seemed good for my family as well. It seemed like it was the first time in awhile we had no surgeries to deal with. Elizabeth was doing great, after her brain surgery she began to train for the New York marathon. She not only finished the marathon but she was also awarded the 2001 Comeback Runner of the Year. Later that day her boyfriend of three years proposed to her in

New York. She called me right away and asked me to be her maid of honor. I gladly accepted. It was a breath of good news after so much my family had been going through.

When I was not spending my time with John, I was still with my girlfriends. We only grew closer over time. Especially Mary, Liza and James (Liza's boyfriend). We all lived so close together and we all were so far from home. When everyone else was going home for long weekends, we always knew we would have each other. Both Liza and Mary were from California and James was from Chicago. John and I also made some other friends. Most of them were just people I would see when we went out, except for Tommy. He was a guy John had gone to high school with but was several years younger than him. We hit it off instantly. He was constantly over visiting with me and Mary, and because he didn't play a sport on weekends when everyone was busy with games or practice, we spent time together. I loved him like a brother and still do. I will never forget him or the friendship he gave me. With him laughter was never missing and that was something nobody should ever take for granted. I know someday, somewhere, we will laugh again.

Christmas came fast that year and before I knew it John was driving me to the airport and saying goodbye. I was sad thinking about not seeing him for three weeks, but I was also excited to get to see my family and my new niece. She was born on November 27th so I hadn't seen her yet but she graced her presence to me at the airport that year. I never realized I could love something so quickly. It was as if she had always been there.

While at home for the holidays that year, I decided to buy a car. The car I had at school was definitely on its last leg so I had arranged to buy a car at home. When I needed to get my car back to school, John offered to come out east for five days and make the trip back with me. I was ecstatic to have him come meet my family and see where I was from. It was weird. I had never let anyone get close enough to want to bring them home with me. For the first time I was sharing with someone where I had come from and the people in my life. But truthfully I liked it. I took him places I only went to alone and places I went to think about him. For the first time I was really letting a man into my heart and home. Everyone in my family got a chance to meet him, and, of course, everyone wanted to meet someone that I was bringing home because it was such an infrequent circumstance. He was shy at first but seemed to get along well with everybody. I realized it was a lot for him to handle in just five days but he handled everything well.

The trip back to school could not have been any more fun. I had never thought so many hours could pass so quickly. We stopped at truck stops, stayed at a dive motel, laughed, and talked seriously about our lives. It was just the enjoyment of good company that seemed to pass the miles. As we neared school, I was actually feeling sad that our trip was coming to an end. However, when we got back to campus, our relationship seemed stronger than ever. Having John meet my family only made our relationship move in a better direction. Without us both realizing it, we were letting people see the love we shared for one another.

It wasn't long after that trip when he gave me the same opportunity to share in his family and hometown. I couldn't believe how far I had come. It was only a month or so later that I was meeting his family at his sister's engagement party. I have to say I was nervous, I hadn't met someone's family in so long. I never got that far into the relationship where I had to do that. I remember I actually threw up before he came to get me. Mary never let me live that one down. But after the forty-five minute car ride and a drink or two, I had calmed myself and was enjoying the party. We had grown so close and our relationship had really evolved into a deeper more meaningful bond.

That spring I was at his sister's wedding dancing in front of a room full of faces that could see us together and how much we loved one another. It was the first time I had been to a wedding where I felt as though I could have been the one getting married, and deep down I thought we eventually would.

Before I knew it I was nearing the end of my first ever spring semester. It all happened so quickly. With my health, friends and John I think I was too busy to even notice until the year was closing in and finals were upon us. It was my first full-completed school year. But more importantly I had completed something that spring that I never imagined possible. I took a class that required us to do a speech about something influential in our life. I tampered with the idea about writing about the rape but hesitated. It was John who encouraged me to do it and let my feelings just reveal themselves in the most honest way possible. I finished the speech and let him read it. I will never forget that moment. He looked at me so sadly. I think it was the first time he actually could see what had happened to me. His eyes were filled with tears, and I could tell he felt hurt. He was hurt that other people could have harmed someone he loved in such a way. After seeing his reaction I no longer hesitated.

The following night I sat before a room full of classmates and professors and read my speech aloud. The room stood silent after I was finished. But the funny thing was, it wasn't an awkward silence. It was the same silence John revealed the night before. A more powerful moment where emotions raced and tears were shared. It was the first time I had told my story aloud. My heart was alive and open for those to see. Afterwards, many of my fellow students came up to me and just hugged me, they probably didn't know exactly what to say to me or maybe they just knew in that moment that was all I needed. With time I have forgotten many of the faces in that class but I will never forget that feeling and that night we spent together. Each one of them gave me something they may never have realized, acceptance and courage. I can only hope deep inside that some of those students remember the story I shared with them that night and maybe even a small piece of me.

It was my greatest accomplishment, and I knew I wanted others to hear the story again. I wanted to touch more people and let them know something about my life. I will always love John for encouraging me to do such a difficult and courageous thing. The spring came to end not only with me finishing all my classes but also accomplishing a truth I never imagined possible. I wanted that feeling to last forever and I feared it wouldn't.

I had already made arrangements to stay for the full twelve weeks of summer school that year, and I was excited about finishing more classes and reaching my graduation day. After classes finished, I moved across town to an apartment in a small complex. There were only five apartments in the whole place and Tommy lived in one of them. He convinced me to live there earlier in the year. He knew everyone else that was going to be living there so it sounded like fun. So I had arranged to live there with a friend of mine. But for the summer it was just going to be me in the entire place since everyone else was not doing summer school classes. After I moved in, I packed my bags to go home for a week. It was all the time I had off in between the end of spring semester and my first day of summer school. In that week I experienced something greater when I became a godmother to Ann's first baby. I couldn't believe I had to leave again so quickly. Coming home only made me miss Cape Cod and my family, but I was still in school mind set from just finishing, so even though it was difficult getting back onto a plane, I fought my tears and focused on class. My only saving grace was knowing I had John waiting for me when I got back.

Even though John had a job that summer an hour away, we spent most of our free time together. I felt like we were living together which I thought would always scare me to death, but for some reason it didn't. I loved the thought of coming home to him at night and spending our afternoons together. When we weren't on campus, we spent time with his family and friends. I was starting to get to know them very well, and being far from home, I loved the idea of being in a family setting. It was a nice getaway from the campus life too. I had a full load of classes that summer, but I was determined to simply plug away and regain my ground. I knew with each class I was taking I was taking a step towards graduation and that always kept me going.

My relationship deepened with each passing day. I was in love and not denying any of it. There were only hints of moments when we were actually apart from one another. I had never known to love someone so sincerely and openly. As the classes came to an end, I returned home for just two weeks. I used my time strictly as vacation. John came out for the last week to enjoy the time off with me. It was a nice break before all the reality of school and classes would start all over again. We spent a lot of time with my family, going to the beach, and just enjoying the Cape. I will admit there is no better place to be in the summer. That was always what I hated about summer school in the Midwest.

There was no beach or water nearby at all. Sometimes I would just feel so land locked. So when I was home, I never missed an opportunity to take advantage of my surroundings. Both John and I used that time to rejuvenate and recoup for what would be our final year of college.

Chapter 13

My senior year, I could not believe I had actually made it this far. I had surpassed my back surgeries and stayed in school regardless of not having field hockey to drive me along. I never thought I would be able to make it through school without my motivation of field hockey. But in life we find other motivations that drive us through our most challenging moments. For me it was my father. After I was raped and dropped out of school, I knew my father felt a different kind of sadness for me. I knew he just wanted me to get my life back, and I knew he feared me falling into a darkened depression that would hold me from doing that. He hated what had happened to me, and I knew he had to do all in his power to not take his own actions because someone had hurt one of his daughters in a way that was unforgivable.

Like most dads he just wanted the best for his child and he always wanted to be able to protect me. But in this particular incident it was beyond his control and I know that ate away at him every day. I know it ate away at everyone around me. My dad tried everything to just encourage options out there for me so that I wouldn't have to feel like my life ended because of that night. With time, when I started working, I could always sense he wanted me to fight back in some way. When I got accepted to the new school in the Midwest, I knew he was finally happy that I had that going for me. I knew his heart broke each time I had to have a surgery, but he admired my strength to go back. I made a promise to my dad that no matter what I would use this opportunity to get my degree. I never broke promises, especially one like that. I owed it to him, and now I felt I owed it to myself.

I could finally see clearly what stood before me. Though with each day I found peace in knowing my time in school was finally coming to an end, I knew something larger was in my head, my relationship. I knew this would be the year that would test our strength and show our true feelings for one another. Everyone around us knew we were now serious about one another, but like all things you cannot simply stay in one place forever, there are sacrifices and decisions that must be made every day. For us it would be graduation, then what? It was the inevitable "what comes next" conversation I so desperately wanted to avoid. I saw so many other seniors go through this and it was always the final test of the relationship.

There was no denying that John was a, simply stated, Midwestern boy who enjoyed the comfort of his family and friends and as for me, well, it was time to go back home again. I knew early that year that I wanted to no longer be away from my family. I had been in the Midwest for four years, and I wanted to be back on the Cape. I didn't know much else, but I did know that. John always eased these fears of mine. He insisted that if we loved one another something would work itself out. And deep down I knew if it meant me moving to the Midwest for good, then I would. I knew love would never let distance be the final say in things, and in my heart I wanted to spend my life with this person whom I had grown so close to. Distance would never be the reason I would let our relationship die. Still, we had classes to focus on, and I tried hard to put these conversations on hold until it was time to make decisions.

Columbus day weekend I had planned to go home for a dress fitting for Elizabeth's wedding. A few days before I left John and I had a fight. I don't even remember what that fight was about now but at the time it was enough for me to not speak to him. I always hated the idea of leaving mad with people, especially him. But I was stubborn and so was he. I drove off to the airport not calling him and him not calling me. I felt sad as I got to the airport. I hated fighting with him and even more when I was not going to see him for four days. Still I remained stubborn as I checked in to the ticket booth. Before passing through security I reached for my bags and there sitting in the distance was John. I started to cry when I saw him. Nobody had ever loved me enough to show up like that. Nobody ever tried to stop me from going or leaving. It was one of those moments that feels so much like a dream or movie you can't help but stop and look for the cameras or pinch yourself. Still, there he stood. I walked over to him and just hugged him. I didn't want to let go. I never wanted to let go. Being with him in that moment was the most alive I had ever felt with a man. He just looked at me and told me he loved me. With that I kissed him and left for home.

It was only a month or so later in November when my sister was getting married, so both John and I returned to the Cape for a week over Thanksgiving break to celebrate. Strangely, like his sister's wedding, again I caught myself wishing it were us getting married. I had thought about it a lot and I knew he did too. But we both had school to get out of the way before any weddings were in order. Before I knew it Christmas had arrived, yet again, and the first semester was over. I had a great Christmas that year. Everyone had decided to spend the night at my parent's. It was so much fun to have everyone together for the holiday. Christmas was always my favorite time of year but I especially enjoyed having my entire family together. The only thing I missed was having John there with me. Every day when we would talk, I only missed him more. About a week before I was to go back out to school, my mom and I took a ride to go shopping.

Strangely she stopped at the bus station, to my surprise I looked up to see John standing before me. I couldn't believe he was actually there. He had planned everything with my mom without me having any idea. So I got to spend the last week of vacation with him by my side. That was the best present I received that year.

We both returned back to Oxford for what was supposed to be our final semester. Even though I was excited about finishing up school, I was falling so deeply in love and I feared our next step after graduation. There were so many days this would be the topic of conversation but neither of us were talking about it. We never made any decisions; we just avoided the reality of things down the road. We were both in classes over our heads but tried as hard as possible to keep things stress free to enjoy our time together. I never told John but really I feared those were our last moments together. I never really knew if either one of us would be capable of leaving home for the other. I suppose only time would reveal that.

Spring break came quickly that year and I had made arrangements to go to Florida with my family. It had been about three months since I had seen them so I was looking forward to some time with them and away from my books. I wasn't prepared for how much I would miss John for those ten days or so. It hit me in the airport when I walked away to get on the plane just how much I did love him. Somewhere on that flight I realized I would be able to move out to the Midwest for him. I loved him and nothing could stop that; well, nothing was supposed to stop that.

I met my family in Orlando where we drove to Vero Beach for a week and then went to Disney World for four days. It was exactly what I needed, some time in the sun and the company of my family. It was a great break. While I was on my way back to the airport, I remember talking to my parents about my relationship. Without hesitation I told them I had met the man I was going to marry. I am not sure they were even surprised to hear that from me. Although I enjoyed my trip, in my heart I was just as excited to return to see John. I came off the plane and practically fell into his arms. It was as though a piece of me could now resume living. I felt closer to him in those moments than ever before. The distance and short time apart only made me want to be with him more. I was no longer nervous about the school year ending; I was excited to begin a deeper journey alongside a man I truly fell in love with. I began to adjust to the idea of us living somewhere together with school and the college atmosphere finally behind us. Who would have thought anything could have stopped my heart from beating so deeply. It was only a week later that my heart fell and broke into a million pieces.

Chapter 14

I was only six weeks away from finals and the end of the semester, and I never would have thought so much could change in such a short time. It was that next week when I found out John, my love, my life, had been seeing his ex-girlfriend. From the time he had told me they had broken up, he had actually been seeing her from time to time. At first I couldn't understand it. I couldn't figure out when he would see her when we were together all the time. I kept asking when this could have happened? I was uneasy and sick. How could something so right be so wrong without me even realizing it, how could I have been so naive? This was supposed to be the man I was going to give my life to, I was going to move for, and more importantly I was going to give my hand in marriage to. What had I done so wrong? I felt empty inside and my heart felt as though it no longer knew how to beat as it once had. I could only say goodbye and walk away alone. Who was this person I had let into my life, who I had let love me, who I had brought to my home to meet my family only to discover he was not true to me.

Nobody can ever capture the feelings in that moment when you discover you have been hurt emotionally. It is a surreal feeling of sheer pain. For an instant it is not real to you and then as you awake, you discover all your sadness and pain is more real than ever and it is now your being which consumes your every minute. I knew nothing at that time, all I knew was I could not be in that small town any longer. So much to many of my professors, friends and family's dismay, I dropped out of school, just five weeks before the semester was going to end, to go home. I remember one professor looking at me as I was tear filled in her office telling her I was leaving; she asked if this was just because of some guy? "Is some guy really worth all the work you have done so far?" I looked at her as honestly as I could and answered, "No, some guy probably isn't, but when it's 'the guy' that is a different story." I sat crying and she consoled me. She knew then that this was different and told me if I ever came back or ever needed help, she was there for me. I will always appreciate her sincerity towards me in that moment.

I needed solace. I needed innocence and like so many times before I knew I could only achieve that from home. My mom had agreed to fly out and accompany me on my long eighteen-hour drive back home. She was one of the only people I could have had with me at that moment. I knew somehow she would be the way I needed her too be. No lectures, no bashing, just company if I wanted it.

I suppose the worst and most painful part was how much John knew about me. He knew my past and how challenging school was for me. He knew how difficult my journey to graduate had been and now he was the reason I was leaving again. This time I wanted nothing to do with coming back, and I wanted to pack my car for the final time never to return or graduate. This was my intention. I was letting go of so much, and I knew I was going to regret it down the road. However, the only problem with all of that is the moment. When you are thrown into a moment, you can only see so much and at that moment all I saw was a small town trying to break me down. For the first time I had lost my will to fight again. I had been defeated, and I had been defeated by a person I had never loved more in my life. He was the first person I had let in since the assault and now he was the first one to simply deceive me. Those days before my mom got out there were unbearable, I couldn't eat or sleep and all I did was cry until I felt I had no tears left in my body.

On one night I received a strange call. It was John's mother. She was crying and I could barely hear her. She begged me to not drop out of school, and she said even her son was not worth that sacrifice I was making. She tried desperately to make me stay. John had told his mom a lot about me even about the rape. For her she just wanted to see me graduate. She had seen me come so far and didn't want me to give up this for her son. She was ashamed of him and apologized for raising a son who could have done that to someone. I appreciated her call and her honesty, but I had already made up my mind and I knew there was no changing that. I needed to go home.

I packed as much as I could fit in my car and left just what I would need to stay for the summer if I changed my mind and decided to come back. It was the only compromise I would make with anyone. I insisted I was never going to go back to school, but still I kept everyone happy and said maybe I would go back that summer just so they would leave me alone. With the right amount of work, I still had a chance to graduate in August if I felt I wanted to.

But I didn't want to make that decision right then. I just wanted to go home and not be in a place where I would see John. Deep down I knew if I stayed I would want to just be with him because he was all I wanted. Even though I hated him more than anyone at that moment, I knew he was still all I really wanted.

My mom was flying in on a Saturday. On Friday afternoon I had a knock at my door. When I opened it, John was standing there speechless. I hadn't seen him for about a week (which was a lifetime for us). With him standing in front of me it all felt surreal. I wanted him to tell me it had all been a bad dream but knowing that wasn't the case made it even worse. I tried to do all in my power to not let him in but I did. I wanted to hear him and what he had to say. I felt I deserved that. Sitting in my room with the walls stripped of their pictures and my clothes packed in multiple bags, it finally hit John that he was losing me. I honestly think he thought he could convince me to at least finish the semester, but that wasn't the case. It was so strange, but even with all that was going on, just being with him was the first time in days I actually felt like myself, but I knew it was all going to end. I didn't want to feel so sad and empty anymore so I let him be there with me and that was the last night we ever spent in that small room...that same room we had talked to each other about getting married in, that same room we laughed and loved one another in was now just a prison cell of our fate without one another.

The car ride home had never been so long. I felt sorry for my mother. She was just there in the car and as we drove, I sank lower and lower into silence until I no longer had the words to speak. Why was I always the one having to leave? Why was I the one always packing my belongings and saying my goodbyes? Nobody could answer this for me. It had become such a routine for me. I felt as though each time that I would fight my way back, something or someone was out to get me.

It had taken my heart so long to love again and John knew that but still he managed to be selfish and now I feared I would never be capable of giving my heart to anyone else again. The heart is such a fragile and confusing thing. It can give so much and then change so suddenly. I felt a million different emotions but not one of them sane; mostly I wanted to be alone. When I got back home, I felt a sense of failure. My one promise I had made to myself and to my father was to graduate, and I had come so far only to let myself be beaten in the end. John tried to contact me but it was too difficult, I couldn't bear the sound of his voice, nothing he said made any sense to me anymore. Strangely enough he was the only one I wanted to talk to and the only one I felt could make my pain dissipate. I guess that is a weird feeling, when you have someone in your life for so long who you depend and rely on in so many ways and then just like that they are gone and we are left with no shoulder to cry on. Although I had my friends and family, I wanted John and I knew I couldn't have that. Why was it that the one person I desperately wanted was the one who was causing me so much pain?

Coming home that particular time was different than any other. I couldn't eat, sleep or barely even breathe. Most of the time I slept for about an hour or so. For the rest of the night I was just miserable and alone. When you stay awake for such a long time, the world seems to function around you as you stand on the outside looking in, like everything is fine without you. Everyone else is fine. Truthfully this is never the case, but I suppose that is what the mind can do to a broken heart. It is almost as if you cannot distinguish between your reality and your dreams. But in times of need, that is what family and friends are for. So I used them as much as I could. It was my mother who finally saw my pain and told me that if the heart really does love someone, it will learn to forgive and grow in its own time. She was right, for now I needed time and what was meant to be would simply be. I guess this was really a test of our true love. I suddenly found my strength each day and with time eventually began to sleep again. When I finally found the desire to answer John's calls, it was mostly ending with tears. He would apologize and tell me he had made the biggest mistake and wanted to spend his life making it up to me, but each time I could not surrender to my inner morals. I valued the trust and honesty in a person too much. I wanted so badly to just go back to him and make the past disappear but unfortunately that wasn't an option. All I really wanted was to know why? But he never had an answer for that. It was usually just answered with silence.

I grew to understand the questions were now for me, could I truly forgive and forget? Could my love overcome anything possible? Confused and scared, I could not answer my endless questions that simply haunted me. Those five weeks passed quickly and when they ended, I only felt guilty for not trying to fight through them with any ounce of courage I had left in me. But that was in the past now. However, I did have some unfinished business to tend to that May. I still had plenty of my things back out at my apartment that I needed to get home. I had decided I was not returning for summer school and I just wanted my things out of that town so I could cut my ties with everything. Even with all the good memories I had at that school, I was only able to remember my final days and I just wanted it to all be over. In an effort to get in my good graces, John offered to drive my things back to the Cape with me. He thought it was the least he could do and hoped he could have that eighteen-hour car ride to maybe get back into my heart. The previous times we did that car ride we were always so happy and some of our best memories came from those trips. So in a moment of weakness and maybe in a glimpse of the past, I agreed to fly out and drive my things back home with him.

When I saw him, I could not help but let my emotions do the majority of the talking and honestly I just missed him. Just being near him gave me comfort like I had never known. In the last six weeks it was the first time I felt alive and breathing again. From the moment I saw him I felt life enter my soul once again. Except I was embarrassed, I didn't want to feel anything except hate towards him, but I couldn't. I was afraid of what everyone would think when they saw me with him. I usually never cared what anybody thought of me but this time was different. I truly was embarrassed and felt like a hypocrite. From the outside looking in, I always thought if someone cheated, that was it. There was no second chance. But I suppose like a lot of things you can never really judge the situation until you are actually in it. So I let myself go and before I knew it we were on our way back to the Cape. We had no idea what would happen when we got there, we just let fate take its course, which it did.

After the drive, John spent a week with me at home. It was so strange; it suddenly felt like old times. It was the most peaceful week of my life. Like we had just met for the first time. I never had even thought about what had happened. I was just lost in my own world with him. It was like nothing we had ever had. Every day we woke up and did something together that we had never done. Even though it was too cold to actually go swimming at the beach we still went everyday. It was still not peak season on the Cape so most days we were the only two on the whole beach. We would sit there for hours. Afterwards we would go out to eat or make dinner at home. It was like we were on vacation and just being tourists together. On one particular day I took John to my all time favorite place on the Cape. It is called the Cedar Swamp. Settled within the dunes of the outer Cape is a trail that takes you down to a swamp. As you walk deeper into the woods you get to a boardwalk that takes you into the swamp. It is the most beautiful place I have ever seen. Everything is so quiet and untouched. As we reached a bench we sat together to take a rest. There in a tree we carved our initials and hid a penny in that same tree. It was such a strange moment. I couldn't believe I was actually there with him and carving something so permanent even though our relationship was still so questionable. I still have not been back to the cedar swamp. My last memories of that place remain in a time I have yet to go back to.

On the seventh day, I found myself having to say goodbye again, only this time I was not the one leaving. John was driving back out to the Midwest to finish summer school and graduate in August. It was the hardest goodbye I ever had to say. It was not only letting go of him for good but it also reinforced the closed opportunity for me and school. I watched his car slowly fade out of sight and simply cried. So much of what I had wanted had just driven off into the distance. I felt I had no direction and no hope for myself. We had spent an amazing week together and yet it felt like I would never see him again. Only nobody could prepare me for the way my heart operated after he left.

Chapter 15

Regardless of much else at that moment in my life, I also felt a deep promise had been broken to a very important person, my father. I still had a hard time looking him in the face after I had let my promise to him fade. With John in my head and my dad in my heart, I made a decision to change that forever. I knew I owed it to my dad to finish school, and I owed it to myself to graduate and keep my goals in sight.

It was a Wednesday when John left and classes started that Monday so I had to make my arrangements quickly. Somehow I managed to get things tied up and talked my mom into driving me out that Friday. I was about to embark on the biggest challenge of my life. I had twenty-four credits to complete and only twelve weeks to do it in. It was almost impossible, but I felt inspired; so with my last grain of dignity, I was on my way. But the even bigger challenge to many was my living quarters. Many people thought I was crazy for my decisions, and maybe I was, but still I went. That Saturday I moved into a small apartment with John, yes that's right John. We were both taking full loads of classes in hopes of graduating that August together. It had been a matter of days when I decided to just up and leave and give my relationship and school its final reign. I was destined to graduate and discover if true love really could forgive and forget.

I truly do believe some of my best and worst decisions come under moments of sheer terror, impulse, and desire. In this situation I was right. I was going to spend the next three months going to class every day and night with only John by my side. We didn't know many people on campus as many of our friends had already graduated or left for the summer so we were forced to spend our time just with one another. But among a sea of unfamiliar faces, his was the only one I wanted to see at the end of the day anyway. It was then I did question love and its power to overcome anything. I don't really know if that is something that really does exist or if it is something we as people have simply manifested into our lives but never really feel at all. Each day was not exactly all seen through rose-colored glasses. When we were good, we were indestructible; but when it was bad, it just became confusing more than anything. I began to question if we were fate or just too people who needed each other right then. Still, there we were living together after the trust had been taken so violently from under my feet. Undoubtedly in these months I came to understand I would always love John because more than anything I loved him as a person. The question remained was could I ever really forget our past and just let our love hold us together. I knew with time this would be the question I would only be able to answer.

I admit I had many insecurities when it came to us. I just felt it was so hard to really trust someone that quickly after everything had just happened. Some days I didn't know if I had made the right decision, and we would fight a lot about that. I knew my thinking was just a normal state after being cheated on, but still I knew with those thoughts we were only going to fight more, which we did.

I turned to my neighbors upstairs and John turned to the few football players he still knew on campus. My neighbors were two guys, Jay and Ben. I met Jay one day as I was coming home from class. John was at his night class so I sat outside with my new friend. We talked for quite a while. He had a girlfriend who he had been with for quite some time. I asked him a lot about relationships and trust. Before I knew it, we had been talking for hours. As I started to leave and go back to my apartment, he said something to me I would never forget. He asked if everything was okay with me and John. I was out of answers and just stumbled to say yes and then ask why? He just looked at me and said, "Because I live upstairs and I can hear more than you probably know."

I was embarrassed and quiet for the first time in our whole conversation. I didn't know how to answer that. The truth was John had always liked to drink. Usually we went out a lot together. But recently I found he was drinking more to hide from us and our truth. When he came home drunk, I knew he would yell and get loud. I was yelling too though. He would say he was coming home and then not show up until 3 a.m. I didn't know how I was supposed to not be angry with this. If he wanted me to trust him, he sure had a weird way of showing it. His actions made me question him even more, and the more I questioned, the louder he yelled.

Our fights got ugly on more than one occasion, and I knew exactly why Jay was asking me that question. Naturally John hated the idea of me having friends that were guys. But I didn't care. I told him I had nobody else at school that I knew; and if I wanted to hang out with Ben, Jay and his girlfriend, he was just going to have to deal with that. I often told John he had no reason to not trust me and until he did he was just going to have to learn to deal with my friends. When we weren't fighting, John would sometimes hang out with us but I always felt he just wanted to scare the guys from getting any ideas about me. You would have thought I was the one who had cheated on him.

Still even after our fights ended, John and I remained together. There was something about us that always brought us back together in the end. Maybe it was just fear of being alone or maybe we really did need each other to get through school and our lives at that point. I remember one night John and I went to a wedding in his hometown where two of our friends were getting married. We had a fight prior to going to the wedding and I almost didn't go, but at the last minute I got in my car and met him at the reception. I wasn't feeling well and stayed pretty quiet for most of the night. As the night went on, I only started to feel worse. I had a throbbing pain in my right arm from a bite I had gotten earlier that week. I didn't think much of the bite on my arm when I left for the reception, but by the end of the evening I was near tears in pain.

John and I were hardly talking so I told him I just wanted to go back to our apartment rather than stay at his parent's. I hated staying with his parents if we were fighting. I always felt bad for them so I would pretend everything was fine with us which I hated doing. I begged John to just come back with me because I was feeling really bad at that point. I don't know if it was his way of just getting me to stop asking him or what but he followed me back to our apartment. When we got back, I was in a lot of pain but wanted to talk to him. As we sat on the couch together, I gave him a gift. I didn't have much money seeing as how I wasn't working, but earlier that day I found an old cigar box and bought it for him. I told him it was something he could always keep things that reminded him of us in. I know it wasn't a lot but it was straight from the heart. When he saw the small gift and my sincerity, we both seemed to forget what we had been fighting about and simply sat there. It was after that I showed John my arm and went to the emergency room. At that point it was paralyzed and I could not move any of my fingers. The doctor didn't know what my bite was from or what was causing the problem so he took out a book and showed me a picture of Shingles, told me that was it, gave me a prescription for Prednisone, and sent me home.

As John and I returned to the apartment at about 5:00 a.m., I looked at him lying in bed asleep and thought to myself we really do need one another. I was thankful to have him there so I laid next to him and fell asleep. So, as much as I questioned what it was that kept us together, that night somehow I just knew I needed him. So, the cycle continued…we fought and then we made up. That was just what we did.

As time passed, so did our three months of school; and early that August both John and I had finally graduated from school. After my last class was over, I wasted no time rushing home to call my father. I was so proud to just tell him that I had kept my promise to him and was now an official college graduate. Amazingly John and I had done this together and I knew without him by my side and I by his, we never would have reached our ultimate goal. School had been my life and challenge for so long, and I had finally touched the light at the end of the tunnel. I was there standing amongst it, shining brightly upon me, I had not been defeated and I knew this was only the beginning. That endless tunnel with infinite darkness had finally cast me through to the other side. To this day I still don't know what amazes me more graduating or graduating alongside John.

Soon after we packed our cars and headed away from college for good. Leaving behind that small town, I only hoped I could leave my mistakes and take along with me all I had learned both in and out of the classroom. I think for myself most of the important lessons that came with me came from nowhere near the classroom, they existed within my daily life experiences and I will take that with me everywhere I go. As I drove away from that small familiar town, I felt sadness at the same time. But I waved a final farewell and accepted the road before me. I was prepared to look into my father's eyes and show him the strength he had taught me. I was finally going home for good, and this time I held my head high and my diploma even higher.

Chapter 16

John and I had decided to have some time to relax before
making any more decisions; we had a busy summer and
just wanted to spend some time in the sun and on the beach.
Looking back at what we had both completed we could
now really appreciate it and spend some quality time
together without the stress of school in the way. We didn't
talk much about our time at school, and we didn't talk at all
about our fights. It was as though without acknowledging
them they never really had to exist. Both Ben and Jay had
told me I deserved better than what John was giving me. At
times I felt they were right but then behind closed doors
only John and I knew everything.

That is the one sacred thing about a relationship. You
have these intimate moments that nobody else will ever
see. And if you keep them quiet, they are always there like
a vault that cannot be opened unless you have the right
combination. For John and I that was all that mattered. We
didn't care about the outside world because we knew how
our own inside world operated. The only delusional
problem with that is you keep thinking things will change

and get better because you are constantly telling yourself that, and you don't let anyone else in on what is really going on. You begin to justify behavior and actions in a way you normally would not do if you were telling your story out loud.

I had never told anyone about the black eye John gave me one night at summer school when he came home drunk. I simply kept it locked up within our vault. It is easy to tell people the good things about a relationship, but it is much too hard to accept the bad things that you want no one else to see. Afraid to let go of what I knew and what I still deemed love, I simply stood by his side through all the good and bad. I used those two weeks at home to forget about everything from that summer and just tried to enjoy my accomplishments. It is amazing how quickly you can disregard the past when you try hard enough. I held onto the past where these issues never existed with John and I and pretended the present actions of his drinking and violence did not exist. I was able to fool myself into loving him and found myself not wanting him to leave again.

But like all good things that come they also have to go, and two weeks later I stood in front of John saying goodbye with no answers in sight. We had barely talked about the inevitable, "what's next," and were going to let things happen as they would. It was the first time in awhile we would not be seeing one another ever day and coming home to each other at night. I felt sad and lost again. Watching someone leave is always hard but that time seemed especially hard because we had no idea what our future held, or if we even had a future to hold on to. Looking back I know it was the most difficult goodbye because such a large part of me knew I should be saying my final words to him. Still, I did not let my brain speak and kept quiet while I tried to just keep my tears locked up inside.

Because of our lack of trust I was petrified to do any sort of long distance. Though John was constantly reinforcing his mistakes and his feelings for me, I still had my doubts and was still trying to heal the deep wound, which remained. I was so reluctant to try long distance at first, but I was also not ready to just say goodbye so I opted to give it a try only if we could start making plans for a change. It didn't take much time apart before I became weary of the distance. I could not get accustomed to not seeing someone I loved. I just felt like two people who have problems with trust should not be testing the relationship waters with distance and time apart. I think even if trust weren't a factor, I would have had difficulties with this, so obviously it was even harder now. And still I was a bit selfish. I felt that since I had gone out to the Midwest for school that John now owed me a chance and risk.

I had always been the one running after him and keeping us together so I felt it was simple enough, this time it was his turn. I felt deep down if he could leave his hometown, his family and friends, I would feel he really did love me. I had followed my heart in the most difficult and desperate times, and I now wanted him to do the same. I was standing my ground and refused to move after what had happened. I felt we needed a new place and a different environment in order for the relationship to truly have its second chance. All John and I had known existed in that small town built on lies, drunken promises, and surreal risks. Now I wanted more, something new, something real. I continued to use the school environment and stress of graduating as our reasons for our rocky summer together and with time it faded from my mind, but not from my memory. With that at hand, I just wanted to try things on my terms for once. It sounded strange, but I did truly feel in my heart that without school and the college setting anymore we could start over.

Still it would take awhile before any move was upon us. It was still early September, and I went to work for my mom once again at our shop. When it was not busy at the store, I would spend my time writing and thinking about the past. John and I had agreed to see each other once a month until he moved out east. So in late September, even though it had not been a month, I boarded a plane to go and visit him. Like many times before, I was anxious and restless for the entire trip until we landed and I saw him there waiting for me. I always loved that feeling in the airport right before I was going to see him. It was always such an unexplainable feeling of happiness. Whenever I am in an airport now, I catch myself looking at the people around me. I see them say goodbye and it still reminds me of how difficult that moment is. Whether it is your family, friends or a loved one, a goodbye is always the hardest thing to do. Then I see the people who are practically running into someone's arms and grabbing one another as if they will never be apart again. I still think the airport is one of the most interesting places in the world. Maybe it is because I had to do all those hello's and goodbye's myself so many times before.

That visit with John went by so fast, I felt like as quickly as my plane landed I was taking off again. John and I went camping in the mountains of Kentucky when I was there. Neither one of us had ever been camping like this before. It was really in the middle if no where and was very quiet and remote. It was so nice to sit around a fire and just rely on each other for entertainment. We talked so much that night. I don't even remember if it was about anything important, it was just the comfortable banter you have with someone you've known for a long time. I always knew if nothing else we would always have the comfort of good conversation. When John brought me back to the airport just five days later, we sat together in silence. I knew we were both thinking the same thing. Neither one of us wanted to go another month being apart. Each time we would say goodbye we always knew exactly the next time we would see one another. It made things easier knowing there was a date in sight.

By late October John was back visiting me. One of my good friends from my childhood was getting married. I had known her for as long as I could remember. I lost my first tooth at her house and we had been through a lot together, the hardest being when her dad passed away when we were in the seventh grade. It was awful. One of those moments when you never know what to say so you just try to be there as a friend. We were so young, and it seemed more like a horrible nightmare than an actuality. I always tried to understand her pain and what she was going through but the truth was I never really could. As we got older, it would dawn on me just how sad she must be at times. I felt bad and just wanted to make her pain go away. The day she called me and told me she was getting married I felt so excited, mostly I was happy just to hear her so happy. Her husband was the sweetest guy and she was lucky to have found someone so perfect for her.

It was yet another wedding for John and I to celebrate together. It seemed the older we were getting the more of that we were doing. Unlike the time at my sister's wedding, I had a different feeling inside me at my friends wedding. For the first time I wasn't picturing John and I getting married. I wasn't wishing it were us that day. I don't know what that was that day, but I knew something had come over me. I still loved him, but I felt a distance between us. At the time I assumed he needed to move there and that would resolve those feelings. So that was what we planned to do. For a couple days after the wedding, we began looking at apartments. It was the first time we were actually doing something that steered us in the direction of being together without all this distance between us.

John was always insisting he wanted to move as well. For him the relationship needed that most. He agreed to move under one last request. He wanted to move only if the past could be left in the past. A new beginning to him meant starting over and leaving our mistakes behind. I understood his concerns and had his desires as my best interest. It was only fair to give and take a little and this was his wish. So with that said we set asail. I know love never comes with guarantees and this was going to be something we would both have to work, on but we wanted to do that for one another. We had been through so much with each other. We had seen each other grow, learn, and ultimately make mistakes, so we needed to keep going forward. And we did. That December John officially moved to Cape Cod.

Chapter 17

There are moments in our lives that will never truly seem real. For me watching John pull into the driveway with all his things that December night was one of those moments. He was there and things were actually happening. I could hardly believe my life at that point. We were going to be living at my parent's house for a couple of months through the holidays and to save some extra money. Neither one of us had been on our own so we could use all the help we could get. John had a job within about a week working for a large lumber company, and I was working as the showroom administrator at a new kitchen and bath design studio.

We worked hard and saved as much as we could so we could move out by February 1st, which is what we planned. After looking and pretty much running away from every disgusting apartment we looked at, we finally signed a lease in a beautiful two-floor townhouse across town from my parents. It was nicer than we could have imagined, and we were so excited to finally have a place of our own. I was a bit hesitant moving in with him before we were married, but rents on the Cape were too high for him to pay alone, and we figured it was just the best option at that point. Plus we had already lived together that summer so it really was no big deal. Unbeknownst to many others, I wanted to live with John to make sure this was what I really wanted. I needed to make sure that this was going to be different from our summer together.

Unfortunately when move in day approached, we were not only still at my parent's house, but I had temporarily moved into the Cape Cod Hospital. For about six weeks I was feeling run down and tired. I had no energy and kept getting sick. I tried to ignore it until one day I collapsed at work and had to be taken by ambulance to the emergency room. I didn't leave until six days later. After undergoing a series of tests and blood work, the doctors thought I had an autoimmune disease, they concluded it was either Lupus or Rheumatoid Arthritis. I was uncomfortable and in pain but was released from the hospital and told to follow up with a doctor who specialized in autoimmune diseases.

I was not to go back to work for several weeks, and was told when I did return, that I needed to go back on a part time basis to rebuild my strength. I was so frustrated, we were just getting ready to make a big move and now I would have little income to support myself. John was as supportive as possible. I felt bad he had to deal with all of this, but he reassured me we would get through it.

So we moved in and I followed the doctor's orders of doing as little as possible for a few weeks. I continued following up with all the recommended doctors in hopes of finding a diagnosis and getting on with my life. However, my symptoms were still very prevalent and now changing. I did my best to ignore them for the time and concentrate on getting settled back at work. I told myself I wasn't sick and ignored any pain from there on out. By April I had gotten pretty accustomed to forgetting how I felt and tried to consume myself as much as possible with work. I was finally taking a liking to my career and learning more and more each day. John and I were still doing well and making the transition from college to work was not as difficult as I had thought. The only problem being we now had money but little time to spend with one another. In college we had all the time in the world but no money to spend. It is ironic the way things work like that.

As much as I ignored my health, I think it was easier for John to do the same. Like a lot of things in life they become easier when just left alone. My problem was that with each day my body was feeling a different pain, a pain I wanted nobody to know, a pain I didn't want to know. It wasn't fair things finally seemed to be moving in the right direction. I had a great job, a great home, and a man who I loved coming home to. I didn't have the energy to deal with anything else, so I didn't. But you can only avoid things for so long before they come back and usually in full circle to haunt you. But like all stubborn Italians, which I proudly am, I chose to continue to ignore it all. So in a moment of inspiration and stupidity, I threw out all my pills and cancelled all of my doctor's appointments. I was a fighter and I knew I could fight my health. I simply told myself I was not sick.

One day in early May I came into work after picking up a counter top off Cape. It was a Friday and nearing the end of the day so many of us at work were feeling the end of the week silliness. Around 4:00 p.m. a customer entered. What caught me off guard, at first, was his age. It was the first customer I had in the showroom who seemed to be around my age. His name was Jacob, a realtor on the Cape who had recently opened his own office with his father. He was also in the midst of fixing up the house he had bought and was looking for a kitchen sink. He was also one of the easiest customers I had ever had. He asked me what I liked and thought would look good with his counter tops, and then just bought the one I suggested. He left saying he would be back to pick it up when it came in. I smiled and said thank you. Afterwards for a moment as I walked up the stairs to my office, I caught myself thinking about this new customer of mine.

When I got upstairs, my co-worker Joy smiled at me. She asked who that was and why was I smiling so much. I ignored her accusation and laughed it off. Only when I got back to my desk I felt butterflies in my stomach. I hadn't felt butterflies from anyone in a long time, and if I did, I never paid attention to it. I ignored it for the time being and simply went home to John.

In early May my sister Ann was scheduled to have a Cesarean section. When I knew I could see my new little niece, I immediately made arrangements to go up after work to see her and my sister. I went up to the hospital and stopped to pick up my aunt on the way. When I got there, she asked where John was. I was quiet and told her he couldn't get out of work. I was so mad at him for not coming. He never missed work, and I had only asked him to leave fifteen minutes early. I knew they wouldn't care but he insisted I go without him, so I did. My aunt and I were very close. I asked her a lot about relationships on that car ride up to the hospital. She had been divorced from her husband for quite awhile and now was with someone for quite some time. They were great together. I never asked much before about what happened with her and her ex-husband. But on that car ride, she told me things I had never known. It was as if she knew I wanted to talk about John but just didn't know how to do it. I remember her telling me to never waste time with someone if you weren't happy because time went much too quickly and you would always regret that in the end. As we got to the hospital, all I was thinking about was how glad I was that John hadn't come on that ride. For some reason I needed to talk to someone or maybe listen to someone.

We got to the hospital where I held my baby niece for the first time. There is always something so unexplainable about holding a baby for the first time. She was so innocent and small. It was hard to think that someday she would go through her own life and maybe have her own questions for me. I only hoped someday I would be able to be as comforting to her as my aunt was with me that day. As I got home to John, I felt bad that I had been talking about him. Truth was I was confused about a lot of things. My health was one of them, and this customer of mine was the other. I couldn't seem to understand why he was still getting in my head.

When Jacob came in a second time, I felt those same butterflies in my stomach. I barely had the nerve to go down the stairs to meet him. The second time he came in we talked about faucets and ordered him one, but before I knew it an hour had gone by and I knew a lot about him. He was twenty-nine years old and had graduated from my high school five years before me. We knew many of the same people and talked a lot about our families and living and growing up on the Cape. It was as if I had known him my whole life. I knew it was just casual conversation, but still, something about him intrigued me. I think it was the way he looked at me. The way he made me feel like I was the only person in the whole room. He seemed truly interested in who I was. I began to feel guilty for even talking to someone in such a meaningful way. I felt like I was cheating on my relationship.

I had always told John, when we first started dating, that I would never be capable of cheating on him because I would be the first one to tell him. I would not be able to live with that feeling of guilt. He and I had been so busy with work that we barely had time for anything else. It was weird he looked at me differently. It was like his mind was on Cape Cod working but his heart was off somewhere else. I tried to talk with him about it many times, but he never really had an answer for me. I just felt guilty from taking him away from his family and friends. I never understood that though. I know he never felt guilty when I was out in the Midwest so why did I? Maybe that was just the difference between us.

Still I confessed to him one night that I felt nervous about our relationship. I told him there was no one specific in my life, but that I had found myself wondering if there was someone else out there. I told him I loved him, and I wanted to not feel like that. I felt something must be missing if I was having these thoughts. He looked at me angry and confused. He didn't know what that meant. I tried desperately to explain to him that I missed our relationship. I missed just being with him. I missed the late night talks, the constant laughter, the silent passionate connection, and our intense desire for one another. I felt he didn't look at me. I was constantly feeling insecure and wondering if he was cheating on me. I knew I was supposed to leave the past in the past, but it had dawned on me that that was much easier said than done.

Even with my truth told John still simply ignored my words like he had done before and continued to act the same. At moments I would see glimpses of our old relationship coming through like a stream of sunlight that fights through a sky of clouds. But it wasn't frequent and I found myself missing him and what we once had. Actions were hard to take since we were living together and he was so far from home. So, I simply silenced my feelings and hoped things would work themselves out.

The summer came quickly and I continued my rambunctious mind set with my health. I went to work every day and followed with a three to four mile walk at night. From what any outsider could see, I was simply a normal and healthy twenty-five year old. What nobody noticed behind closed doors was the truth. It started as fatigue but raged with intense pain. A deep throbbing pain that left me at moments feeling paralyzed. At first it was just a muscle spasm here and there that would last for about a minute than subside. They were manageable and never debilitating and usually by the next day I was fine again. A good nights rest left me feeling rejuvenated for the next day. Still, I saw nothing major wrong and just kept walking because it was all I knew to do to clear my mind.

At first it wasn't evident to me why John ignored my health and left it sleeping inside of me. When I would cry at night or wake up in pain, he simply turned his head or consoled me for a minute then went back to sleep. I loved his ability to deny the same way I could. With neither one of us paying particular close attention to how I was feeling, we didn't have to stop and face any harsh reality. But eventually silence rages too loudly and the force of ones mind soars in another direction, usually when things become unbearable. I couldn't stop questioning our relationship. We were not dealing with my health nor were we dealing with a lot of things, and I found myself in a state of hate and regret from our past.

Suddenly I felt I didn't know who I was coming home to anymore. I was so afraid he would hurt me again and I was constantly questioning him. I knew it was difficult for him to deal with but I could not help my mind. It painted the most outrageous thoughts and stories when he was not in sight. It got to the point where I did not even trust him to go to the grocery store.

I found myself thinking about other people out there, other people who weren't capable of hurting another in such a way. Did they exist? That was all I wanted to know. I wondered if there was someone out there who could simply love me as much as him but without all of the heartache in between. Was there someone who could be happy just loving me and only me? This solemn thought drove my brain into a craze. It kept me awake at night and haunted my day. While I walked it was all I thought about. Again Jacob kept making his way into my thoughts. He was still coming into the showroom, and I couldn't get him out of my head. Honestly I wanted a chance to get to know him better. I just wanted to see him outside of work.

I knew in many ways John felt me drifting away. The distance we had overcome was now there more than ever. I felt his fear, but I wanted to be honest with him and I never wanted to hurt his heart. We agreed some time apart might be needed. Unfortunately we couldn't just take a break, we lived together and had a deeper commitment. So in an effort to save what was left, he agreed to go home for ten days to give us a break. I knew we would never have all the answers in ten days, but we needed to try something. I had not kept my promise and was letting the past haunt me every night.

When John left for home, I told him I wanted him to act as though he was single and I was not in his life. I told him to see his friends, see his ex-girlfriend or go out on dates. I didn't care. In my eyes he was single and so was I. I knew I was asking the impossible, but I wanted him to see his life after college without me in it. Granted I knew ten days was never really going to be our answer to one another, but at this point we had nothing to lose. We were already losing the relationship so any last effort was worth it in my eyes. I used my time to do the same and finally agreed to go out with Jacob. I had been honest with him from day one about my relationship. I knew all too well how lies could affect things in the end, and I didn't want to mess anything up with him even though I had just met him.

Jacob used to call me at work practically every day since we had met, asking me out, and every time he was given the same response, "Thanks for the offer but I have a boyfriend." After awhile I think he just asked to ask even though he knew the answer beforehand. Obviously you can guess his shock the first time he asked me out and I said yes to him. He came to pick me up, and I had that same feeling the whole time until I opened the door. He took me to a restaurant I had never been to before. We talked so much that it was about forty-five minutes before we even ordered. We stayed until the place was closing, and we had to leave. I can't remember what I ate that night, but I do remember it was the best first date I had ever been on. As I was getting up from the table, I noticed the picture that hung on the wall above our table. It was a picture of a man and woman and underneath it read, "The Proposal." My heart literally jumped as I grabbed my purse and followed him out the door. He drove me home and said goodnight. I hated the idea of the date even ending, but I went inside and barely slept. I had that anxious, excited feeling you get after an amazing date. The feeling that you don't want the sun to rise because then the night will officially be over so you cherish every moment of darkness as you relive every moment of the night.

I continued to go out with Jacob for that week. Even though I felt guilty about John, I knew I had to take advantage of my time if this is what he and I had agreed to do. So I put my guilt to rest and went on my next date with Jake. He took me on a boat over to Martha's Vineyard. I hadn't ever been there so I was excited to see the island and spend more time with him. When we got to the island, we took a walk so he could show me around. It was beautiful. The sun was still shining and there wasn't a cloud in the sky. It was the perfect setting and seemed unrealistic to me. We had dinner at sunset in a bar overlooking the water. Sitting under the warm night sky, deep in conversation, I didn't even realize how late it was getting. After stopping at one last place for a drink, we headed back to the boat. When I got home that night, I felt like I was on a cloud. Who was this guy who was literally sweeping me off my feet?

We spent that entire week with one another. I often wondered how this looked from the outside, but only for a second. I felt I deserved to be taken out and treated like this. It was romance in its highest form. Unlike a drunken bar scene, we were enjoying each other in ways John and I had not done. We were so used to bars and constant drinking, but with Jake it was more romantic and enchanting. I felt like a princess. As the week neared an end and Jacob and I were out on our last night, I felt sad. I didn't want that week to end. I didn't want "us" to end. I knew I needed time to figure out my life with John, but I also knew Jake was now a part of my life too.

Now being sick I had a different perspective on things. I realized if something was in fact wrong with me, I wanted someone by my side who I could trust would never hurt me. Being sick enabled me to see that John may not ever be that person. When he cheated on me, I had merely six weeks before I decided to go and live with him. I never had enough time to truly cope. In many ways I think I went back to him because I was afraid I would never love again. I knew how difficult it was to love anyone at all after I had been raped, and I didn't know if I could go through all of that again with someone else. In my own selfishness I attached myself to all I knew in fear I would never know how to love like that again. When John returned, he came home to open arms but a closed heart. I had realized in such a short time that I at least needed to know I could survive on my own before just accepting what he had done to me and living with it.

Still he did not want to believe our relationship was over. I tried to open my heart to him one last time but within a week I found myself packing a bag and walking out the door. I told John I couldn't do this anymore. I knew I wanted the romance. I wanted the fearless relationship with someone who loved only me. I didn't want to feel insecure to who he had cheated on me with anymore. It was breaking my heart down. In the week I spent with Jake my heart felt alive again in ways it had never felt. I told John I was tired, tired of fighting for us, and tired of always waiting for him to follow me when I walked out on him. The truth was, whenever John and I fought, instead of yelling at one another I had the habit of walking out the door. I had done it so much it became an expected thing when we fought, and he knew eventually I would always come back. So he never once followed or chased me out the door and told me not to go. I admit it was all I wanted. For once, I just wanted him to walk out the door behind me and tell me he loved me and to please just stay. That night I walked out the door and waited in my car. He never came out, he never told me to stay. He let me go just like that.

So with that, I found myself at my parent's house. They weren't surprised to see me at their doorstep when I knocked. It was like they had been waiting. I told my mom I was just done with everything, and I needed to leave for good. I wanted to start over. I didn't know where things would go with Jacob, but I knew I needed to give my heart a chance. I felt like John in that moment. All I could think of was when I first met him and how he had this past and how I begged him to just give us a chance. It took him one year to finally decide he wanted to take that chance with me. I knew I couldn't do the same. I didn't want to lose a chance with Jacob. He deserved a chance just like I did. I knew his situation all too well, and I wanted him and I to have a fair chance to make things work.

When I spoke to John, he told me he just wanted me to come back home but I was insistent that he had already let me go and now he needed to leave. We played these games for a couple weeks, and still in that time, never once did he come and fight for me. I had a hard time believing if he really loved me that he would just sit and wait for me to walk through the door. I was angry that I meant so little but it only proved to me that he was not willing to chase me. Still he was not leaving as I had asked him to. I told him if he wanted to stay, then he could have the apartment but we were not together. If he wanted that, he would have to work at that. Inside there was a part of me who at least wanted to feel him fight just so I knew he loved me at all. But after his two-week notice was given, he was finally packing and ready to leave the Cape and me.

John had asked if he could see me before he left, and I was a little weary to the idea. I felt what was done was done, and we needed to move on. Seeing him now would never have any benefit. So I went to work knowing that Friday he was leaving for good. I don't know if it was love or a moment of weakness but after work I drove into the small apartment complex and watched from afar as he packed his car. I sat there crying. I was not only watching someone I loved leave, but I was watching a part of my heart being taken away in that car. No matter what anyone said a part of my heart was still feeling sad for all it had gone through. I picked up my cell phone from the car and called him. As we spoke, I was crying. We kept talking as I entered our apartment. As I reached the top step, there he was standing before me. Both with phones in our hands and tears in our eyes we said nothing and hugged. I hadn't seen him in four weeks. I hadn't felt his touch in even longer.

There was so much to be said but neither of us said anything. I spent that weekend with him there in that apartment that was once our home. We ordered food from our favorite places, talked, and lay beside each other just in disarray. On Saturday night we sat outside on the back deck. The sky was full of stars and it was so quiet. I asked him if he regretted anything. He told me his biggest regret was not following me out the door that final day I walked out. We didn't talk about fixing anything anymore, we just enjoyed our last moments together. We made a promise that night that a year later to the day we would meet each other at the Cedar Swamp. It was such a typical thing for us to do. Constantly setting up the next time we would see each other to make it feel less final. I knew I would never see John again but just setting that date somehow made the moment that much easier.

On August 29, 2004 John packed his things and drove back home. I had no answers for him. I just knew I needed to be away from him and us right now. It was not fair of me to be with someone whom I could not keep my promise to. I felt I had deceived him and my guilt ate me inside. I hated myself for having to let him go, but I knew I honestly had not forgiven him. Plus there was another promise I had never kept with John. When he found out I had been raped, he wanted me to get counseling. I had tried it in the past and hated every minute of it, but he thought I needed to let things with my past go before we went forward. I never in fact did this for him. I was sorry I hadn't. I was sorry for him, and I was sorry for myself. I had so much to figure out with myself before I could attempt to figure out my life with someone else, and I told that to him. I needed to figure out me and "we" were just going to have to wait. I knew this was a risk, in letting him go now, we may never be together again; but I also knew I needed to take care of myself before I could take care of someone else. I never knew I could cry as much as I did the day John went home. Again saying goodbye to my best friend and my love only to accept myself and keep my promises alive with me.

I spent days replaying my time with John and how things could have been better, even trying to go back and pinpoint where are mistakes were made. I was tired of it though. I was tired of figuring things out. Especially when I never got anywhere. Still, a piece of my heart remains with him and probably always will. He was my first true love and my first true heartache. His memories will somehow always live within me as they do with many people in our lives who have impacted us in ways we never knew possible. I couldn't help but remember that day we spent at the Cedar Swamp about a year before. I caught myself wondering about that penny. It was such a symbol of our relationship. There it was, so small of an object battling the weather and still trying to remain strong. When he drove off that day, I wanted to go back and see if that penny was still out there withstanding all of nature above the simple letters, which symbolized "us."

I never went back to the cedar swamp and still haven't to this day. I suppose it is too painful. I see a lot of things in life as fate, and I know how to read signs because I believe in them. Seeing if that penny was there would have been too much of a sign, and I don't think I could have ever prepared myself for the answer whatever it may have been. I may never tell this story again, and it may even be silly and childish, but I guess that is why I like it. My void in the world, my John, I may always question what went wrong and if I could have fixed it but for now I am just happy to have known I was capable of loving one person that much. For that, I will always be grateful. It is an amazing organ, the heart. Just when you think you cannot open it more, somehow you learn to forgive, somehow you learn to live, and if you are lucky, you learn how to love. My final words as John left were simple..."I love you." It was as simple as that, and we both knew it.

Chapter 18

I had my life to figure out before me. I was single for the first time in years, living alone, and trying to remain healthy, the latter being the most difficult of them all. The roommate situation was quickly resolved when I purchased my new best friend, Wrigley, my wire-fox terrier puppy of just six weeks. He quickly added noise around the now quiet apartment and was a good distraction from my obsessive thinking about my health and relationships. After John left I knew I had a call to make. I knew when I told Jacob I needed time to figure things out, he would respect that. But I also knew what he wanted more than anything...he wanted his chance to show me what a real relationship with him would be like. So I called him. He immediately asked me if John and I were back together. I was crying but laughed and told him no, he was gone and it was over. I told him I wanted us to take a chance. I wanted to let my heart speak, and it did with Jacob. So I needed to listen to that.

Jake later told me that phone call, where I told him John was gone, was the best moment of his life. He said he was shocked and excited. He had thought he was no match for my four years with another man. I eased him by saying it may have been four years but it may have been with the wrong man. Jake and I spent a lot of time together right away. We seemed to be moving quickly only it didn't bother me. It was the first time in so long I had the chance to see what a difference trust can make in a relationship. John and I never started with any trust, and we ended with even less. With Jake I was discovering how easy it could be to open one's self when you have trust in each other. I was not hesitant to tell him anything, and I found myself wanting to tell him more each day. There were so many things we shared in common and loved about one another. Because he was older I knew his aspirations as far as a relationship were concerned were much more serious. He was twenty-nine and not looking to play games or just be with someone for no reason.

At first I thought I wasn't going to be able to give this to him but strangely I did. He had my heart faster than anyone had ever before. He had met my whole family and friends, and I had done the same with him. Normally, I was so scared of this, but with Jake it was just so natural. He was so gentle and kind that it was impossible for anyone to dislike him. At times I wondered how I deserved someone so amazing. There was so much we wanted to do together. Talking about the future just came in and out of conversation so easily. I had never been so wined and dined in my life. He was just a natural with me. We had so much in common. Especially when it came to past relationships. Jake informed me his last serious girlfriend, who he had dated for three years and was planning to propose to, had cheated on him. It had been three years since the incident, and he told me he just wasn't meeting the right people after that. He too had his issues with trust, but he taught me how to not carry that into your next relationship. He would tell me that not everyone cheats or not everyone will hit or yell at you. He helped me stand high with myself and gain back some of my self-respect that I had so violently lost.

It was everything I had wanted, so naturally I wanted nothing to change that could ruin this chance with this amazing person. Unfortunately for us, we could not avoid the larger issue on the horizon, my health. I had tried so hard to hide my health from Jake in hopes to keep it out of our relationship. I did not want to start our relationship with something like that but sometimes you have little choice. It was not long after that he saw, firsthand, my health slowly slipping and fast. Unlike John, he did not ignore what lie before him and he could not turn his head. At first I resented his interest and pressure for me to go to the doctors, but I soon grew to understand even I could not defeat the inevitable.

Suddenly my daily walks became more of a hassle than an enjoyment. I was not going everyday sometimes only twice a week and for only about a mile or so at a time. Afterwards I would come home only to cry in sheer pain. I felt as if I was in someone else's body. I grew weak and tired but I didn't know why. Work became a chore, and I was lucky to make it through a full day. My legs would have muscle spasms and give out on me. Still I knew I had to work so I put my walks on hold and saved my energy strictly for that. Soon after, Jake noticed a change in my energy. It was when he caught his first sight of a spasm that he felt fear. Nobody had seen this before but John, and I was afraid if Jake saw who I really was, he would leave me and I couldn't have handled that. My heart was too weak. However, I sold him short because he didn't go anywhere. He wanted me to get better, he wanted me to face reality with him by my side. I didn't know how to respond. I wasn't used to someone wanting me to deal with this.

With my best interest in sight I took his advice. First off, I told my parents how I had been feeling. Then I went to see another specialist in autoimmune diseases outside of Boston. With both my parents and Jake with me, I was certain the doctor would be able to tell me finally what I had. Be it Lupus or Rheumatoid Arthritis, I was ready to just start dealing with my life. Unfortunately, he had no answers for me other than that he was certain I had nothing of the sort. I will never forget his words to me. He said, "Such a beautiful girl, but such a bigger problem." He told me he was certain I did not have an autoimmune disease, and he was even more certain and concerned that I may have a muscular disease.

As I left the office and saw Jacob and my dad who were waiting outside, I could barely speak. "So what did he say," my father asked. I took a breath and told him what the doctor had thought. My father seemed as nervous as me. He stumbled on his words and tried to comfort me by saying there was no way I had a muscle disease. I wanted so badly to believe him, but I feared that it may be the case. Leaving the doctors that day, I have never been so scared. Prior to that I had done my reading on both Lupus and Rheumatoid Arthritis; I was prepared for either, but not prepared for something else. How could I have a muscle disease? I was twenty-five and an former athlete. I was just walking four miles a day a few months prior. Something had to be wrong. I felt sad that day. Everything in my life up to that point I was able to control in some way or another, but this was now fully out of my hands. It was now I knew what true defeat felt like.

With my family close by and Jake still by my side, I continued to see more doctors but things were getting progressively worse each day. I spent a week in the hospital outside of Boston where I had no ability to walk and could barely use my muscles. The doctors had thrown everything at my parents as to what they thought I could have. Everything from ALS, Multiple Sclerosis, Parkinson's Disease and basically every other muscle disease out there. I had first noticed this back in July when I went for a walk and came home with a cramp in my right foot. After that, they would come and go. Sometimes I would have a full-blown muscle spasm, other times it would just cramp up or feel irritable. Eventually those cramps moved from my foot, into my right leg, and then into my left foot and into my left leg until it just took over my entire lower body. I felt so ashamed and naive for hiding this for so long especially since I couldn't walk. I hated myself for that.

I was transferred by ambulance to a rehabilitation clinic near my home after my stay in the hospital. The hope was to get my muscles to function again. I had completely lost the ability to walk and was in a wheelchair. My first days at rehab I was put in a machine that would brace myself in a standing position to try and get any movement in my legs. The first day I hung lifeless and unable to do anything. As I looked around the room, there were so many other people there trying to get better. I was the youngest patient at that time, and I felt like I was making the worst progress. I felt so helpless. I just wanted to be working and having fun with my new relationship. Many times I would try and work from my hospital bed. It wasn't much, but I had started to design now so I wanted to check on my customers. I felt bad leaving them. I never liked the feeling of leaving my work for someone else, and I tried to still focus on getting better so I kept work talk to a minimum. I forced that energy to try and walk again. I was starting to forget what that felt like. Even though I was getting good at functioning in my wheelchair, I knew I didn't want that to be the case.

I will never forget the first time they strapped me into a machine that lowered me into a pool. When I got in the water, my therapist unbuckled my safety belt and let me stand up. In the water I was so buoyant that I could actually walk again. I was running all around the pool so happy to have my muscles working. The only bad thing was as soon as I was lifted out of the pool the walking stopped. Still it was a moment of hope. Things had happened so suddenly. My spasms were now lasting anywhere from ten minutes to hours at a time. Afterwards, I was left feeling lifeless. I stayed in rehab for about two weeks until I regained the use of my legs and was able to walk only with the assistance of a walker or loft strand crutches. I remember just feeling so happy to be able to walk at all. I felt like I had met my goal and made so much progress. I was so thankful to everyone there who supported and assisted me in reaching that goal.

The crutches and wheelchair were just a temporary fix until I felt better to be back at home. Still the thoughts of living in a non-handicap accessible apartment, scared me a bit. I knew my road to recovery was just starting. But still I was fearful there was no road at all. I feared this was now my life. I was under the care of some of the best physicians in the state, but no one could seem to link my symptoms to any illness. I was a medical mystery to many. It was obvious my body was doing something, but the tests were not linking anything together. I felt at a standstill.

I was only working minimal hours to simply cover my health insurance and trying desperately to focus on just getting well again. With my money running low and no answers in sight, I began to lose hope. I felt confused and lost. Where was I going next? I pulled from every depth of my soul for that competitive fighter to just come alive and defeat my body but it never worked. I went many days not working and barely walking. Sometimes at night Jake would have to carry my lifeless body up and down the stairs. I was incapable of living on my own because I could no longer take care of myself. For the first time in my life I was afraid to even be left alone.

Luckily, my parents were undergoing a full renovation at their house so they moved into my extra bedroom at the apartment. It was great, I really needed the extra help at home and it helped them out too. The timing was actually perfect. I did feel sorry for Jake. I mean here I was still in the first months of dating and now my parents were living with me. It never bothered us though. We actually enjoyed them. My mom still managed to give us space when she thought we needed it, my dad on the other hand was content sitting in the middle of us on the couch. Even though my mom tried to drop hints, he still didn't get it. But truthfully, Jake and I just laughed at it. They were great company and the best help for me. Sometimes I don't know if I could have done that without them there. They will never really know how grateful I was for that. As much as I thank them, they never will fully understand from my point how lucky I did feel to have them in those months.

Chapter 19

With my health still at a standstill I felt hopeless. The hardest part was looking at this man whom I had only met several months earlier dealing with all of this with me. I tried hard to look at it from a positive mind set. It was truly a test of the relationship only I was growing tired of all these "tests." I always felt like a burden to Jake and my family. With little use of my legs, I was not able to drive and needed assistance for everything. I had my new puppy that I could no longer even walk. It would break my heart to look into his little eyes and not know if I would ever even be able to take care of him. I guess that is what families are all about because my family never failed to be at my side through anything and neither did Jake. Whether it was the dog, bills or needing a ride somewhere, they never failed. A few weeks later the spasms were moving into my arms and hands. It was as though someone else had full control of my body's function. Mostly I was scared. I knew a little about the muscle diseases out there, and the thought of actually having any one of them scared me to death.

Months passed with no answers in sight. Each day I grew more and more tired as my energy level plummeted. Most days were spent at doctor's offices up in Boston or on the Cape. My days were consumed with new doctors every week only nobody had any answers for me. My mind grew tired to the point of no return. The only red flag that seemed to appear over and over was the rape back in 1997. Some speculation had risen that all this was due to the rape and the mental and emotional stress of it all. Many were convinced I had not yet dealt with everything, and my body was experiencing post traumatic stress syndrome or a conversion disorder. I was familiar with the disease but was deeply certain it was not the root of my illness. Still I followed the doctor's orders and finally got counseling. I saw an amazing doctor whom I spoke very openly with. We unraveled the past and even the present. But after weeks of appointments, he was certain my illness had nothing to do with the rape and was not any form of stress related incident. It was as though there was a conflict between all of the doctors. And in the middle, I was left just getting worse each day. After seeing a counselor I liked I couldn't help but feel I had kept a lost promise to John, I was finally seeing someone and talking about my past. I knew he would have been proud of me for that.

I grew tired and weak from laying in bed. I wanted to find someone out there who would just stop and listen to me without assuming my past to be the root of all that was happening to me. Unfortunately that took awhile. The holidays came quickly that year. Although I always loved that time of year, this time it was different. I was afraid I was slipping further and further away. I wanted to feel something else. With my family and Jake still alongside, I tried to ignore the fear that existed deep inside and simply enjoy my time at that moment. Unbeknown to everyone else, inside all I wanted for Christmas was some kind of an answer. I wanted to simply know I was going to get better. More than anything I wanted to know I would walk again. I wanted to know what I had so I could learn how to fight it with every ounce of strength in my body. The unquestionable doubt ran deep in my head and I needed to get away from it.

Jake and I spent the New Year that year at his parent's place in New Hampshire with the hope of getting away and getting my mind away from everything. It was a beautiful condo right on the mountains. It was the first time I had been away and out of the house in months. Though I was slightly afraid to leave my comfortable surroundings, the change of scenery really lifted my spirits. For three days I tried hard not to think about my health and just enjoy the time at present.

It is always a weird thing when you know everyone is worried and thinking about the future but they try so hard to simply ignore it. It's as though the conversation exists but nobody is really listening. That is how I felt a lot of times. However, no one could deny the positive in my life, Jacob. A man who stood beside me day in and day out and never gave up hope. Some days I knew he was more afraid than anyone, but he had this way of only being supportive. Occasionally, people would ask how he was doing with everything, and he always answered humbly that I was the one they needed to be worried about. He spent many days up all night with me sick. Some nights it felt as though we never slept because of the constant pain that kept me awake. When I didn't sleep, neither did he; and when I would awake in pain, somehow he would be there too. We shared many nights simply in tears as he tried desperately to just ease any of my pain.

I don't think I could ever know how to thank him enough for all of that. I mean here it was still the beginning of the relationship and we were forced to take things more seriously. I suppose it was my ultimate answer of his feelings towards me, still I feared being hurt.

When news spread of my health, John caught word and the next thing I knew I was sitting on the phone with him. I never hid that from Jake. I wanted to always be honest with him about my relationship with John and when he called to check on me. Because Jake and I had met so suddenly and amidst everything, I wanted him to know I was always being truthful to him. John admitted he felt lost without being able to help me for the first time in his life. He told me it was so hard having to sit back and let someone else do what he thought was "his job." I couldn't help but question his intentions and if he really was sincere with those words. It was obvious he felt hurt I was already with someone else so soon after our relationship ended, but at the same time I couldn't help but think he never did anything to prevent that.

On my birthday that June before John had left, he gave me a gorgeous ring. He knew how much I loved crowns. And from the time I met him I always had worn that cheap silver crown ring which I had given him. He used to always take it off me and play with it while we talked. He would say someday I am going to buy you a real crown ring. I would just smile and tell him I liked my cheap silver ring. The day he left I gave him the ring and told him I wanted him to hold onto it. I told him I couldn't have it. One night on the phone when I cried to him about my illness and everything going on, he told me to get off the phone and get some rest. Before I hung up he told me to look inside the top of my jewelry dresser, which I never opened because it had stuff on top of it. I hung up the phone and lifted the top on the dresser for the first time since I had gotten it. Inside was the ring he had bought me with a note that read, "This will always belong to you. Love John."

I couldn't help but think if he was so concerned now, then where was he? Where had he been? If he was so concerned why was he just calling, why was he not there? It reminded me so much of our past and how I always had to be the one fixing things and chasing him. I guess in many ways I felt it was my turn to be chased. Months passed with John still calling here and there to touch base and catch up. Mainly it was about my health. But each time he said he wished he could be the one by my side. I could not help but be reminded about our past and how in many ways he wasn't really there when I needed him most.

I have always hated the idea of comparing people against one another, and I didn't want to do this with John and Jake, but sometimes I couldn't help it. There was so much about Jake that seemed surreal to me. He was so caring and "perfect." I felt I was missing something. How could someone be this nice to me? Especially with how little I could offer him at that present time. Here we were spending everyday in and out in my apartment just waiting for something, anything to happen. Weekends came and went with me in bed and in pain. What Jake never realized was that many of the tears I cried in those moments were for him as well. I was so sad to see him just giving up his life for me. It broke my heart to see him just there through everything. At the same time all he could say is that he wanted to be there and would have it no other way. I wanted so badly to believe his words and I had no reason not to. Well, just one reason, my lack of trust in basically everyone.

I knew my health was not due to the rape, but what I never denied was how the rape affected me in so many ways and again especially with relationships. A day had never passed where I felt that I could truly trust people. I knew this was difficult for Jake. Here I was using my past and John as an excuse to pull away from him. Each time we got close I feared his intentions and I had no reason to do that. With John I suppose the worst had already happened. I figured he had already hurt me and it would be impossible to do it again. With Jake I knew I could never risk going through any pain ever again. But the truth was I needed him. I needed Jake in ways I never needed anyone before. I had gone months without seeing John, but I had a hard time going a day without seeing Jake. I found myself needing him more and more everyday which was the biggest difference. I wanted to make sure I didn't just need him because I was afraid to be alone and incapable of taking care of myself. I wanted to know if I needed him because, regardless of my illness, I just loved him. This was the next issue I knew I needed to clear in my head. I knew I needed to really understand myself on my own before I could involve anyone else in the picture of my life.

Chapter 20

Things took a turn in February when I found a more westernized doctor who felt he could help me. I wasn't in his office long before he had a diagnosis for me. He was certain I had Lyme disease. I recalled back to that bite on my arm back at summer school that was diagnosed as Shingles. Months later they discovered I never actually had Shingles but still I ignored it and never thought much of it. The doctor felt I may have had the infection from that bite, and the infection had been undetected in my body for about two years. Which was exactly about the same time frame that I had been having all my health issues. It was the first thing that actually made any sense at all with everything that had been going on.

I had been tested several times for Lyme but on each occasion it came back negative. About 99% of the previous doctors and current doctors who were seeing me, disregarded it and felt no desire to simply try the treatment to definitely rule out the possibility. I distinctly remember the first time I was put in the hospital my mother asking the doctors to just put me on the antibiotics, but they refused sted it was just a waste of time. Truthfully speaking the Lyme medication is just a very high form of antibiotics so there is little risk in trying this medication. At this point I was so frustrated and focused on getting better I would have tried anything, and I was just happy to have someone with an idea and game plan for once.

The medications were to be taken for eight months, and then after that it would be reviewed to see if I should continue to be treated or if I was getting better and nearing a full recovery. The funny thing with Lyme is that it is different in every person's body and that is true with treatment as well. Some people respond in different ways to different antibiotics so there was no guarantee with anything. With the Lyme in my body, if in fact this was what I had, it looked like a chronic case which meant it would actually never leave the body but could be treated with expected bad episodes or flare ups, periodically.

So I left the office that day ready to try something and praying in my heart it would just work. The following week I continued to see a movement specialist north of Boston. In my heart I just wanted her to conquer that Lyme was the diagnosis and be on my way. That night she informed me she wasn't certain I had Lyme Disease and was interested in looking at things more closely. She did think there was a possibility I had Lyme Disease in conjunction with something else. She did ease my mind and everyone else's mind when she told us I did not have ALS, but she still had other tests and treatments she wanted to try with me. I was open-minded at this point. I felt comfortable with her and was ready to listen to the suggestions she had for me.

She put me on a drug that treated me for a dopamine deficiency. She was treating me for a disorder called Dopa-Responsive-Dystonia. I was put on a small dose of a dopamine drug and then told to slowly work the drug into the body. Of course, another medication with all the fun side effects. I was on so many pills at this point I could barely keep them straight. Each one had the infamous nausea side effect. So many days I had a hard time even keeping any food in my system. But I simply ate what I could eat at the time and tried not to think of my head hovering over a toilet. The new medicine would also take awhile of monitoring before anything was known for certain. So again I left with at least a possible diagnosis but no certain answers.

By the end of February, I at least felt confident in my treatment options and just wanted to start getting my life back in order, only that wasn't the case. Because I had only been working on average 30 hours a week, I sensed a problem on the horizon with my health benefits. The company had been good up until that point, and I knew I couldn't expect them to continue this for much longer which they didn't. I got a ride into work one Thursday morning from my mom and was prepared for my two appointments, which were coming in late that morning. While organizing my notes and proposals, I was taken into the conference room. (The conference room was in the main showroom with no doors and open to any customers who may be in at the time.) I felt certain the conversation was going to be about my benefits. Only it wasn't.

Out of the blue the company had decided to let me go. With my appointments still scheduled I was being told to leave that very day. I was so thrown off guard. I had been with the company from the first day and had always been a hard and reliable worker until my illness, and I was still managing thirty hours a week regardless. I was not offered a part time position with the option to pay my health insurance, I was simply let go just like that. I did all in my power to try and say something; anything, but I was speechless and could only struggle to hold back the tears that raced down my face. Even worse, customers were now in the showroom witnessing the situation and I still needed to track down a ride home. I grabbed my crutches and stood outside waiting for Jake to come and get me. I had never felt so hurt and small. Just another bump in the road that I knew emotionally I could not handle. Up to that point in time, work had been a healthy distraction for me, and I new without it I would go crazy inside.

I suppose to fully understand my anger and sadness I should add that my best friend's family owned this company. We had gone to high school together and been through a lot of good and bad times together. We had known each other for over ten years. When I got sick, she decided to help out at the showroom as the manager. When she would come visit me in rehab, we would talk about work and what needed to be done. When the time came for her to take on her first managerial duty, she hid in fear and let someone else do her dirty work for her in letting me go. I was sad that a friend could have this ability inside her. I suppose my naive thinking at least expected a warning more as a friend than a boss.

I had even made a proposal to my father, who works for a building company, about sending his clients to our company for installation of their kitchens and bathrooms to help out the company, and here they were doing this to me. I had one of the highest sales revenues even while I was sick and had more jobs lined up for down the road. I guess what bothered me the most was the lack of options given to me. When I first got sick, my office was on the second floor. Many days when Jake would pick me up he would have to carry me down the stairs or it would take me ten minutes to just get my body to my desk. I begged for months to have a computer set up on the first floor especially when my doctor told me he thought I should have a wheelchair while at work to help save my energy. But it never happened until about six weeks later. Nothing was ever made handicap accessible until it was too late. I will never really know how much more damage I may have caused by forcing myself to do those stairs each time I was at work.

I had many clients whom I just had to leave with no explanations. I felt bad the way such a large company was handling a sick employee. Nobody at that company will ever truly know how much that hurt me, but I hope each day they have a sickening feeling deep inside from knowing how morally discriminatory their actions were. I suppose the worst part behind it all was when I saw an ad in the paper a few days later for my position. Rumor had it they were interviewing one of the employees best friends for the position. When I was let go, ironically, they also told me they did not have the money to keep me on staff at that time. I always thought when a company does layoffs, technically, they are not even supposed to be able to hire for the position they let someone go from. Maybe I am wrong and maybe just bitter, but I suppose the manner in which the whole action occurred hurt me more than anything plus the fact that I lost a best friend over the whole thing. Maybe it was another test of how true friends really are at heart. For myself it was just another example of how trust can be so difficult for me.

Looking back I did gain one great thing from my time working at the showroom, meeting Jake. Also I did manage to make a very good friend. Joy was a woman in her early sixties who I had worked with for about a year. In our small little setting it was easy to get to know your co-workers even if you didn't want to. She was a true romantic. She was remarried to a man who was undergoing a lot around the time I met her. It was an instant connection for us. Her husband, Bob, had been sick for quite some time. Every day was a juggling act with how he was doing, and I was amazed at her ability to take charge with his illness in order to get answers. I never imagined making such a good friend so quickly but she really helped me out. She took me under her wing at work and was always giving me tips on how to handle doctors. When I lost my job that day in February, I later received a call from her. She felt terrible for what the company had done to me and said she couldn't stop crying afterwards just thinking about it especially the way it was handled in front of customers and other employees in the middle of the day. I knew she felt terrible and just wanted me to know she was opposed to their actions. I appreciated her support on the matter.

Afterwards I did not speak to Joy for a few months although Jake and I thought about her often. About three months later, I ran into someone from the company who told me Joy's husband had passed away a couple weeks prior. My heart sank when I heard the news. That night I called her and we talked for about three hours. I felt terrible and I wanted to be there for her. She had no family close by and didn't know many people except those from work. Jake and I would have her over from time to time but there was always a sadness to her that would make me feel so bad.

She had told me so many times before that when she met Bob she knew she was going to be with him. They had a connection that was unexplainable, and they had never really fought in all their years of marriage. She used to tell me that was what she saw with Jake and me. She would say our love for one another reminded her of herself and her husband years before. She had always wanted me to take a chance with love and was so happy when I told her that I did. She was even happier when she would see Jake and I together and just how happy we were. When he wasn't around, she would tell me how she knew we were supposed to be together from that very first day we met.

When I eventually had the chance to meet Bob for the first time, I felt as if I had known him from the stories Joy had told me. I could tell simply by looking at him how much he loved her. It was the way she looked at him, when he didn't even realize it, that I could see just how much she loved him back. I was amazed to witness such a true love right before me. Often times, when I would feel bad about being sick and Jake having to take care of me, Joy would tell me not to worry, she would say that when you love someone it is not a job or hassle. It is something you do purely out of love. It really made me realize what she was saying. I still know my dear friend's heart is broken beyond repair and may never fully recover, and all I can say to her is that I am here for you and only hope and pray in some way that is enough.

Chapter 21

With no job to occupy my mind more than anything and my health still not improving, I was now struggling to find any explanation for all the constant sand that seemed to be kicked in my face. I couldn't help but think that every time things seemed a little better they always had a way of getting even more challenging. I felt like I had nothing. Was this all just a test of my strength? If so, I was ready to quit. I didn't want to fight anymore. I kept trying to tell myself others had it worse, but I also could not help but feel as though for me this was all pretty bad. I wasn't looking for pity but I just wanted to be angry for a while. I wanted people to just understand that things were only getting worse and my morale was slipping. Usually I could always find some positive in any situation, but I was having a hard time at this particular point. I was desperately trying to find something within me that made things okay, but I was always feeling empty inside.

It is a difficult thing when you cannot find something to hold onto for guidance. I wanted my faith, but I began to even doubt that. I wished my grandfather were still alive. I wanted to just sit with him and ask him for advice. He always had the best way of answering things for me. I don't know what it was but he had the best way of looking at life, and I just wondered what he would have been saying to me if he were there with me. Luckily, for myself, God may have heard my prayers and they were answered in a most unusual way.

My neighbors, Lucy and Alan, were an older couple who never doubted anything when it came to their faith. They were very active in the church community and had been more than concerned with all my health setbacks when they heard what I was going through. They asked if it was okay to come by one night to give me something. I was pretty much bedridden at this point so my mother, Jake, Lucy and Alan were all beside me. At this point my muscles were affected in my legs, arms, hands, neck and even in my chest. They told me a story about how years ago they had gone to Lourdes in France. Lourdes is a very well known place where people with debilitating diseases and handicaps are cured on a daily basis. For decades people have traveled long and far to experience the power behind their Holy water used for healing the sick. The water had been with Lucy and Alan for 27 years, and they wanted each of us to join in prayer and take some of the water to help in the healing of this mysterious illness. After saying several prayers together, we all shared some of the water and prayed to God for some answers and healing. Alan and Lucy had been praying for me for months, but they felt the Holy water may be worth trying and I was not reluctant to try anything at this point.

The following week Jake had arranged a trip for the two of us to go down to the Florida Keys where his parents had a house on the water. My doctors thought the warm air might help with my spirits and being in the water would help my muscles move in ways they were not able to move in for four months now. I was excited and nervous all at once. But I listened to one doctor in particular who told me that I should take advantage of this time to get away because the future was so uncertain. So we hopped on a flight and the sunshine and warmth of the Florida air graced us just three hours later.

It felt refreshing to be doing something so fun and getting away for a week. After all Jake and I had pretty much done nothing since my illness had taken over my life. I tried my best to not focus on my health as much as possible and take advantage of each minute away with him. I was so happy to see him being able to do the same for once. We went out to dinner, fished, swam, and took boat rides. It was a true escape from everything at home, and I hated the thought of having to go back. But I didn't dwell on it and just enjoyed my time away with good company and no doctors.

Sometimes I find the best medicine for many people can simply be the freedom of routine. At home I was constantly at the doctors or in bed. When I saw people, it seemed like all we talked about was my health. It became so mentally depressing for me. When I was in Florida, it was truly an escape from everything. I started to mentally take my mind away from my illness and simply focus on where I was and who I was with. I remember one night I felt good enough to leave my crutches in the car. As we walked into the restaurant, I reached down and grabbed Jake's hand. It was the first time I was able to do that in so long. That night when we got home, we listened to music as we sat overlooking the water. Before I knew it, we were dancing together. It was such a romantic moment and something we weren't ever able to do before because of my illness. Although it was such little things we were both so happy because they were small signs of some improvement.

Strangely enough by the end of the trip I noticed I was using my crutches less and less. I was still getting sick, but I felt something in my legs coming back in a way I had not known before. I hated to leave. I was afraid getting on that plane would only lead me back to a time I didn't want to be in. I tried hard to think and tell myself I would simply not allow myself to be sick when I got home. I wanted to take those small strides I had made and carry them with me off that plane and back home. So I returned with a tan, souvenirs, and a new found fight for the challenge in my body.

We returned back home a week later rested and rejuvenated. With each day that passed from then on I started to see something changing. I was taking my crutches with me less and even doing the stairs on a more independent basis. I felt my body coming back to me. I couldn't believe my own eyes. It was as though every day I was improving and noticeably. I was afraid to even acknowledge it at first so I tried not to pay attention to it. But deep down I was smiling larger than life. I no longer felt afraid to be alone, I felt independent and self-sufficient. With so many different medicines, I had no idea which one was helping, and I didn't care. I just knew I was feeling alive again.

At that point I was taking 60 pills a day so who knew what was doing what, but I knew I no longer felt like I was facing my own death, which I had felt on so many occasions before. I remember telling Jake several times that I had felt as though this was going to be the way I would die. But suddenly I felt like I was reborn all over, I felt like myself for once. I was even driving again which gave me back that sense of freedom and broke down those cell walls that I once called my home.

On one day out to my car, I saw Lucy going inside. She looked happier than I had ever seen her. She said she was so glad to see me walking and doing so well. I smiled back at her, and as I walked away, she told me how she really did have faith I would get better and that the Holy water may have given me back the strength that I had lost for so long. As I left that day, I felt a breath of faith restored in my soul. Maybe beyond everything the prayers and water did start my recovery. It sounded strange, and who knows, maybe it was all of the new medications I had started, I guess nobody really knew what it was. All anybody seemed to care about was that I was myself all over again.

I couldn't stop this feeling inside. I wanted to do so much. The best feeling may have been the first time I was finally able to walk Wrigley by myself. We made a habit of walking more frequently together. I was not used to having company on my walks. Usually when I was walking I was alone and simply sorting thoughts in my head. At least that was how it used to be. But now my walks were different. There was this living being right there with me. Sometimes I would wonder if he was thinking, and if he was, what was it about. If you are a dog lover, you always believe your dog is thinking something intelligent. In our eyes they can be the most insightful one in a room solely because they are capable of listening. When I was alone with Wrigley, I was always talking to him. I used to think if he could talk right now he would probably be telling me to just shut up for once.

One night when I was alone at home, I took Wrigley out for his nightly walk. As I started out, I felt a feeling in my legs that overcame my every motion. I started to run. Both Wrigley and I ran as fast as we could. I ran so fast that my legs felt as though they were going to fall right off my body. Both Wrigley and I did nothing else; we just ran, that was it. I felt like a child. Like I couldn't run fast enough. I felt like those kids I once saw on the playground at work everyday. Just running to run, with nothing in sight. My legs wanted to keep going. They had been so damaged and suddenly they felt free again, I felt free again.

I continued my walks with Wrigley, but every other day, I began going back to my familiar walking territory from that prior summer. It was so surreal at first. I felt like I was dreaming. Not only was I back but finally I was doing what I knew so well before, walking. With every step I took, I could not help but feel slightly nervous that this was all a dream I would merely awake from with time. I feared it was just a moment and before I knew it I would be back in bed. But I put my thoughts of health aside and tried to just think about each step. Unlike before where I walked with goals in sight, for now I was just walking to walk. I didn't want to ever take that for granted. I was mentally writing in my mind how far I had come. I could only hope my steps would simply continue with each day and maybe further by the next but for now, if nothing else, I was just happy.

Chapter 22

With my new found independence I came to sort of a realization in my life. I was seeing things clearer than ever. I realized I had an amazing man by my side, but I wanted to discover what I wanted for myself. I took some time to explain to Jake how I wanted our relationship to take a step backwards so I could reevaluate my life. With my health in the right direction, I wanted to make sure I was where I wanted to be and doing what I wanted. I was twenty-five, with no job, but feeling better. I no longer felt like I had to just feel trapped in this life. I felt like I needed to get happy with myself. I needed to see if the Cape was where I wanted to be, if Jake was the man I wanted to be with, and what I wanted to do for a living. I felt like I had so many decisions to make, and I knew I needed time to answer those questions on my own without anyone by my side. I knew before that I needed Jake to take care of me, but now I was taking care of myself so I needed to step away from him and see if I really needed him for the right reasons. I needed to know why I was holding onto my past and John. I needed to know why all these things were happening to me and where they were leading me too.

With my heart in my hand I was haunted by words a friend had once told me. The best advice I have ever gotten. She told me before I could ever expect to be happy with anyone else, I needed first to be happy with myself. Her voice rang loud in my head then and always will. I knew Jake made me happy, but I didn't know if I was truly happy with everything else in my life. I needed time. I suppose my illness and getting better needed to happen because I needed to really look at things from the outside and not just accept myself with a dependency on others for the rest of my life. I wanted to know I could survive on my own. I wanted my heart to have time to heal. I went from John to Jacob to getting sick and all so quickly. All I really knew I needed right now was to see if my own heart could talk to me without any distractions in the way. Things had been so cloudy for so long and I wanted to pray for time. Pray for the time to reveal my sky and what lay amongst it. So there I was waiting to hear a final diagnosis about my health, trying to find my career, and trying to listen to my heart. I felt, truthfully, I had never really given my heart the opportunity to speak, I had merely been caught between asleep and dreaming as to what may come next. I did not know what remained around the next corner, but I knew what I needed and I knew no matter what I was just going to continue walking.

Chapter 23

In an effort towards taking my next step, I began typing.
I would walk each day mentally speaking aloud every
thought in my mind then I would go home and let
everything pour out on paper. It was an escape from
everything else in my life. I was not only writing about my
life and my experiences but I was reliving my life. The
nicest part of writing is exactly that. It enables you to go
back in time and really live all the moments you remember
over again. Be it the good or bad moments, I suppose for
myself I was writing about the most influential times that
truly tested and shaped me into the person that was sitting
there typing in front of that screen.

After a couple of attempts to work, I found my body was
not exactly ready for a forty hour work week with the stress
that accompanies it. My doctors agreed. They felt no rush
was necessary for me to test the waters so soon. Of course
they weren't the one's actually sitting at home trying to pay
bills and not go crazy from boredom. Still I was a sitting
duck waiting fearfully that my health would slip from me
again, so unwillingly I took their advice and filed for

unemployment. I have to say, looking back, it was a smart decision. Unemployment was at least some form of income, and with the summer months around the corner, I was going to be able to use my parent's pool for therapy and really try and recover. It was the first time I actually let myself take a mental break from the everyday routine of work. It took me awhile to realize it was okay to not work. I was so afraid of what anyone else would have thought of me. But after a few weeks, I redirected those thoughts into a daily routine of trying to get better.

Continuing with my writing I was able to see things a bit more clearly. I understood why certain things had happened in my life and how those incidents led me to that exact point in my life. I tried to let my heart speak which it did in the form of Jake. I had realized how amazing he was. At times I felt unworthy of him and I never knew why. He was my angel. I had questioned many times the way he simply fell into my life at a most awkward time. With my relationship just ending and my health starting to fail, I often wondered why did I have to meet him then?

It took some time for my stubbornness to fade, but when it did, I saw things right for the first time. I understood that I could never question or answer why the timing with Jacob worked in the way it did. I simply had to thank God each and every day that I had met him at all. I also could not continue to ask God why he came to me or why I deserved him. I needed to know that we were deserving of each other and that he had not found me, we had found one another.

I thanked God for sending such a person into my life, someone who looked at me with truth and integrity, someone who I could stand before with all my flaws revealed and still feel he loved me even more for doing so. I had never known anyone who could stand beside me through such hard times after only a couple months of dating. In my heart I felt he was my miracle. I needed him more than I had ever needed anyone else, and I knew he felt the same in return. It was as though I had finally understood why my life had taken the course it did.

There are so many times I have thought about picking up the phone and calling John simply to thank him. After all, if it had not been for him cheating on me and us moving in together on the Cape where I had the job at the Showroom, I may have never met my angel that day. Who knows where I would have been. Possibly somewhere out in the Midwest missing my family and questioning John's every move each time he walked out the door. I never did thank John, but I hope someday he will read my words and understand the reason we were together was simply for me to meet the man I wanted to marry. It is strange how fate works, but I choose to not question it anymore and simply try and live with my deepest thanks at heart knowing my fate led me into the arms of my soul mate.

When I looked into Jake's eyes, I saw sincerity, something I had not seen in years. What I thought was sincerity with John was masked by his guilt. I knew in my heart I could never go back to that because of our past and how much he hurt me both mentally and physically. His drunken excuses for yelling and threatening me were far too deep in my wounds to ever heal. For a time I thought this was simply all I deserved and it was okay for John to drink and take his anger out on me. It wasn't until years later, when I had to run out of the apartment in fear of him, that I came to believe maybe it was not what I deserved but merely what I had chosen.

There I was just sitting and waiting to be treated like his little toy that he could come home to when he wanted and treat however he wanted. My biggest fears were the nights he never came home as expected only to show up in the early morning hours drunk and angry. I was so used to being afraid of him that I became immune to it. That was until that day I looked at myself in the mirror and staring back was a black eye and swollen cheek bone. I had let him get me. I knew on many occasions that John had a very serious drinking problem, and as much as I tried to justify this with him, he never listened or tried to change. Looking back I suppose I was not a good enough reason for him to want to change those habits. Maybe his spoken "love" for me was just not enough to want to change.

I am a firm believer that if a person is wanting and willing to change then they can. If in their heart they have found something or someone to love in replace of those habits, then they will inevitably change for the better. It is unfortunate that many of us try to stay with someone even after they continue to say they will change but never do. How is it that we have such a low self-image to just accept what we are dealt. Someday I knew John might have the ability to make a great husband or father, but it was just not going to be with me.

It wasn't until I met Jake, on that off day in May, that I saw for the first time someone who was incapable of those actions. He was there to comfort and console me and I never once feared him. He became my soul mate, my best friend and the love of my life. With each day I only grew to love more and more about him. With that in mind, John began to slowly fade into a blurred memory of how my life would have been, and I was so thankful.

I do really believe that we have parallel lives which exist for all of us. It is the life we did not choose simply living along side of us as a constant reminder of what would have been if certain decisions weren't made. For me it was Jake coming into work that day. Possibly for John it was the day he decided to cheat on me or maybe the first time he hurt me physically. Unbeknownst to many of us we disregard these parallel lives and just continue living in the life we have chosen. But at many times there can be moments or even seconds where we stop and imagine what our parallel life may have been like. For myself, it happens when I look deep into Jake's eyes and feel safe and comfort. I realize in these moments that in some other life there were no eyes for me to look into, just empty vessels from a man I thought I knew, a man I thought loved me. I am only thankful to have had the opportunity to meet my parallel life and act so bravely upon it. Still, as if mesmerized at times, we all may think about those other lives we could have been living. For many there may be deep regret in our choices but for myself there is nothing but sheer joy and gratitude. For I have made a choice, and now I live never in fear but merely in the essence of peace and in the arms of a man who loves only me and I know that.

Taking a risk with your heart may be the most challenging decision a person has to make in their life, but for me it proved only to be the better suited choice and a much better life. Every person's heart has stories to tell which deeply reveal their character. I do firmly believe the heart is the truest sense of reality to one's life, and it can never erase the memories that do exist within it; but if you find true love, those memories are simply put to rest in a graveyard within our souls. We can go there to visit what we once had, but for most of us we just let them rest in peace.

Chapter 24

With the summer coming to a fast end and Labor Day now upon us, I was amazed to see how fast time was eluding in both my mind and body. Things were happening within me once again that were unexplainably different. It was as though I had reached a plateau in my health. I was, however, having some new feelings I had never experienced. After spending the summer really working and concentrating on getting better, I was now reaching a point that I hadn't expected.

For starters, my vision in my right eye was occasionally giving out on me causing temporary blindness. At first I ignored it until it became too obvious too ignore. I had fallen several times due to it and even ended up in the emergency room one night with a sprained arm. Following that were the painful migraines that would leave me in the fetal position and unable to even move due to the level of the pain. And then there was the issue of my memory which had significantly begun to change. It was mainly short term but very apparent to me as I had never had any such problems prior to then involving my memory. I suppose my breaking point with my memory came one day when I found myself in a store and could not remember how I got there or what I was doing there. I even walked around looking for Jake or my mom because I wasn't sure if I was alone or not. After an hour or so, I came out of it and told myself I was no longer driving anywhere.

The new developments eventually led me back to my Lyme doctor who concluded that we had reached the maximum level on this particular antibiotic I had been taking, and I would need to use something different and stronger to hopefully kill more of the disease in my body. The current medication was failing in many areas. After speaking with him, it was decided I try a stronger medication in hopes to kill more of the Lyme that was in my body. In many instances, with Lyme disease, the patient can reach a level where they are still infected with the disease but are no longer getting better or worse. It is as though you have developed an immunity to the antibiotics.

My doctor told me that if I stopped treatment at that point, I would eventually just level out and stay at one plateau with my health. Even though I was having so many good days, I was having relapses in my treatment where all my symptoms would reappear. I couldn't stay in that state. So I was going to try a new antibiotic that would hopefully continue to pull the rest of the Lyme bacteria out of my muscle tissue and help with my symptoms.

The luckiest thing I had for me throughout my illness was my support network. My uncle was not only my godfather but also a true savior. He is a doctor in the Washington, D.C. area. His main focus for many years was with the research of the AIDS virus. Some days I was just fascinated by his sheer intelligence. He was my ear that listened to everything the doctors were telling me. He had copies of my labs and hospital visits sent to him just so he could answer questions for my mom, dad and myself. Sometimes the doctors can intimidate their patients, so my uncle was a good one to ask further questions to because he would be able to answer them and without any "doctor talk" mixed in.

I called him with everything, and he became such a good friend to me. He even accompanied me on several of my doctor's visits. When he finally saw how much my body was being controlled by this disease, he began to take an interest in Lyme. For years he had known about it but was preoccupied with AIDS. He told me once on the phone that if AIDS did not exist, Lyme disease would be the #1 epidemic. He also said if they spent an eighth of the time researching Lyme as they did with AIDS, they maybe would have already found a vaccine.

It was just still so new and un-researched to the depths it needed. There was so much nobody knew about it but needed to be studied. Having my uncle as a shoulder to lean on only helped me to feel slightly less crazy and able to re-capture my patience with everything and the doctors. I knew I needed to let them have their time with me, and no doctor would ever fix me overnight. I loved my uncle for his time and dedication towards helping me even when he had so much to deal with in his own life. To me he was the poster definition of how family should be. He even went above and beyond the call of duty, and I loved him for being so caring and doing that for me.

So after consulting with my uncle on much of everything, he was in sure agreement with the course of actions mapped out by my Lyme doctor. So following my appointment, I did exactly what the doctor had said and went on a new medication. Luckily the summer was dwindling away, and because my new medicine was not sun friendly, I needed to be inside for most of the time and be very careful in the sun due to the increased sensitivity from the medication. Things were progressing along fine until about two weeks later. After a night out to dinner with my parents, Jake and I returned home to what we thought would be a relaxing Friday night. What we did not expect was a late night ambulance ride again to the hospital.

After dinner I came home and was sick throwing up to the point where I could not even stand up. Curled in a ball on the floor of the bathroom, Jake came in and picked me up laying me down on the bed. I was drenched in sweat as my body convulsed in spasm. Only this time was different. My muscles tightened deep in my chest and then up into my throat. Normally I was able to talk to Jake or whoever was around when I would have a spasm but for the first time I was speechless, literally. My throat felt as though the air was being taken right out of it. I knew this was a different kind of spasm, one I had never felt before. As we arrived at the emergency room, the spasms only worsened. I tried to stay calm and focus on my breathing but I was scared, with each moment passing I felt less and less able to breathe. It was the most fear I had felt in awhile.

Laying in the small emergency room surrounded by my parents, Jake and doctors, I felt so far away from everyone. Even in that small room I felt miles away from anyone. I felt no one could help me. After two shots of morphine, two shots of Dilaudid, and two shots of Adavan, the spasm still remained. It was enough drugs to put me into the next planet but not seize the spasm and my body was covered in a sweat that would not cease to quit. Everything was beyond my control. It wasn't until fourteen hours later that my body finally gave in and went to rest.

WHILE I WAS WALKING

I was admitted into the hospital for one week, and unlike other times in the hospital where I had no diagnosis at all, my time this stay mainly revolved around getting my legs somewhat useable again rather than a constant blur of testing. At that point I had already had every test done and the only thing that seemed to come back suspicious was my elevated ANA and my Lyme titer, which my Lyme doctor said showed significant positive bands of the disease. All I was holding onto was his faith reassuring me I was not crazy and did in fact say I had something wrong. I held that faith with me as close as possible. I barely remember my stay at the hospital because of the amounts of drugs they had to give me every time I would spasm. Each time I would spasm would only make me further from walking because it just continued to damage the muscle tissue. My blood work from that stay showed I had sprained all the muscles in my body.

After a week I found myself returning back home to my apartment. I was confined for quite some time to that upstairs bedroom because of the stairs and was mentally just trying to stay somewhat sane from everything that burned in my heart. I was tired from everything. I was tired of being sick, tired of not having a job, tired of having no income, tired of waiting for answers, and tired of just not feeling better. I think the roller coaster ride of getting better and then getting worse was sometimes harder for me. With my mind set it was just too difficult. I would want to fight and go back to walking and driving. I started getting really good at lying in bed, and I hated that more than anything. That apartment slowly became my prison, and the only thing keeping me from not going crazy was again the support group I had from my friends and family. My good friend Mark, whom I had know since the second grade, planned a lunch visit with me once a week. It was a nice thing to look forward to, and I cherished the time we spent in just meaningless chit chat and gossip. I never held it personal that he did break up with me in the sixth grade for Beth just because she had bigger boobs than me. Even though I never failed to mention it every chance I could, we were friends nonetheless. I looked forward to seeing him all the time. He was single and had just moved to Boston so I think I enjoyed living vicariously through his stories.

My girlfriend, Laurie, also became a regular at the apartment. She was practically my third roommate. We would laugh and joke that Jake was actually the third wheel when we were all together. I had met her when I went to high school. She and I were instant friends. We shared the same interest in sports and played on the same field hockey and basketball teams for three years. I was devastated when she went away to a private school our senior year. We remained in touch on and off after that. But when I went to school in the Midwest, the truth was I lost touch with a lot of people from home. It is never intentional when these things happen, for me it was simply the fact that I only came home about twice a year and most of my time was spent with my family since I never got to see them.

People always have the best of intentions of staying in touch when you leave high school, but the truth is, you somehow just fade apart. Still, I was so happy and lucky to have both of my childhood friends back in my life, two such great friends who were there helping me through a very difficult time in my life. They were a constant reminder of who I was when I was healthy, and it made me want to get better just by being with them. Simply by them knowing me as an athlete fueled me with an unknown sense of desire that made me want to be that person again. For some reason, I hated the idea of anybody who knew me as an athlete seeing me now. I hated them seeing me in bed, and when I got out of bed having to use the wheelchair to go back and forth to the bathroom, it hurt too bad. For some strange reason it always made me feel sad and almost like a failure.

It is weird how a disease can do that to you, how it makes you feel guilty for something even though it is nobody's fault. It wasn't until I got sick I realized how much I needed people like this in my life. They were my shoulders to lean and cry on, and I only hoped they understood how much they were appreciated. I really believe it is much more meaningful to have a few true and honest friends than a thousand acquaintances who you never see and could never really lean on like the way I did with those two.

My angel was my sweetheart, Jake, he never left my side, through everything he was my constant. Truthfully I never understood how he did what he did. You expect your parents and family to help you when you are in need but he was always going above and beyond his call of duty. He was up with me when I did not sleep, he held my hair when I got sick, and he carried me when I was unable to walk. When I felt down, he could sense it and he tried everything to just put me in a better place. I never went to bed without silently thanking God for bringing him into my life. When the apartment became too difficult for Wrigley and myself to live in, Jake openly invited us to move in with him.

I had always been hesitant about living with someone after my last experience and I told myself I would never live with someone again unless I was married, but my heart was not afraid. Jacob had pretty much moved in once I got sick so being around each other was nothing new for us, plus I already had gotten accustomed to his messy habits and was prepared to try it. He owned a house a few miles away that was 100% handicap accessible. Plus Wrigley would now be on the same floor as me, and Jake even fenced in the yard so that I would be able to let him in and out of the house on my own.

So it was decided that Wrigley and I would move out by the end of October and move into our new home by November 1st. Much to my surprise, moving was nothing of ease. I had accumulated quite an amount of stuff in my apartment during my near two year stay and it all had to be out and into Jake's house. Being a homeowner for many years, he had his fair share of things, as well, so combined, we had enough for two houses let alone one. After a very stressful week of multiple car trips, the majority of my apartment had been vacated. Thanks to my Mom, Dad and Jake who managed to do the majority of the moving, I was finally settled in November.

Seeing my apartment, with the walls stripped and nothing inside, I could not help but think about how much of my life those walls had seen over the course of those twenty-one months. The emptiness and hollow cold feeling within those walls made me realize that all that was left of my relationship with John was exactly that, empty. It was simply an empty vessel of which would now be left alone to someday be taken over by someone else.

It reminded me of one of my favorite songs written by Ani DiFranco. In the song she talks about a couple who live in an apartment and she says, "I am walking out in the rain and I am listening to the low moan of the dial tone again and I am getting nowhere with you and I can't let it go and I can't get through...the old woman behind the pink curtains and the closed door on the first floor she's listening through the air shaft to see how long our swan song can last...I am watching your chest rise and fall like the tides of my life and the rest of it all...in each other's shadows we grew less and less tall and eventually our theories couldn't explain it all and I'm recording our history now on the bedroom walls and when we leave the landlord will come and paint over it all..." With that song in mind, I took a deep breath, and closed the door behind me as I left behind yet another chapter in my life and prepared to embark upon the next.

I was excited to finally live somewhere with Jake where the memory of John did not exist. No matter how hard I tried to forget John, the fact was, when I was in that apartment, his ghost still haunted me in ways and I was unable to forget and I was finally glad to let the ghost of him die among those same walls we once lived in.

Chapter 25

The transition into my new home proved to be a very simple one. The biggest difference I saw with my relationship, more than anything, was the strong friendship and just enjoyment of each other's company that we shared. When we were home, we were always in the same room. We did everything together. During the week while Jake worked he would check in on me from time to time throughout the day. Not only on the phone but if he had any free time, he was coming home to see if I needed anything or just to say hi. We did everything with one another because we had so much in common. Even when I was not feeling well and incapable of doing anything but move from the bed to the couch, he never complained and he never left without me. We even made the best of having dinner in bed if we had to.

It was what I had always envisioned in a relationship only thought did not exist. We rarely fought, and if we did, it was usually over some small mundane thing that would resolve even faster than it began. We had a great home together and now an even better relationship. This is what drove me each day to get better. I wanted a chance to live a life with Jake without my health being such a constant factor in everything. I knew I may never actually get that dream in a full capacity, but deep down it was all I wanted.

After completely settling into our new home, Jake and I spent some time working on the house and doing some renovations. I tried as hard as possible to help in any way I could. Mainly I would do some small painting where I could sit and take a break when I needed to. The week or so before Thanksgiving we took a break from everything and tried to just plan on enjoying the holiday with our families. Fortunately, both Josh and my parents lived very close to us so we were able to have an eating decathlon that Thanksgiving. It started at about 2:00 PM and ended around 9:00 PM. Looking back, I don't know how we did that. We were both so fortunate to have our parents so close to do so and even more fortunate to have such good relationships with our families.

My family has always been such a large part of my life. I suppose that is why, even when I used to dream of living somewhere else, deep inside I could not imagine being so far from the one's I loved. I had already done that when I was out at school and it was just too hard. There were far too many days I felt sad just not being able to be with them for dinner or an outing to shop with my mother. It is so true when people say the grass is always greener in someone else's lawn.

All of my family was now within forty-five minutes of each other, and though I didn't see my sisters every day, the fact of the matter was I loved just knowing I could when I wanted or needed to. If there were one thing I would never take for granted, it would be that. It is always such a great idea to think about moving somewhere else, but when you actually are that far away and you know you have no family near, it can be the most difficult thing to get used to. I always hated when I would get that sinking feeling of really just being alone and knowing I was too far to just get in my car and be near the people who knew me best.

One of the hardest things was when I would go months without seeing my family and then I would see my niece and each time I saw her she looked so different. It is an amazing thing how we age with time. When we are around people every day, it becomes harder to see; but when you are away from it, suddenly you can actually see how time works. The first time my niece said my name, I could have cried right then. I knew then I did not want to miss anything else.

Sometimes when my whole family would get together I could not help but catch myself looking around the table. Suddenly, there were my two brother-in-laws and these two little ones. It can be so surreal to see your family grow right before your eyes. Not having any brothers growing up I was excited to finally get to have two. Both my brother-in-laws were so funny with me, I always thought they really did see me as a little sister. They were protective and supportive, and I finally was getting the chance to see what brothers were like to have around. But they didn't have much of anything but amazing things to say about Jake...everyone did. He truly was a saint.

When I met Jake, I felt an immediate connection with his family. They were so kind and caring towards me and with my illness. I never had any problems being with them, I enjoyed every minute of their company and felt lucky to have such a great family in my life. It was so apparent to me how he had gotten the way he was, it was simple...it was who he was from the start. Meeting his family allowed me to know a part of him I did not know, it allowed me some insight into his childhood and how he grew up. It only reinforced how similar we were and how much alike our goals and morals in life were.

For the first time I felt relaxed. I felt I had found a home with someone I loved and even better it was near the people we both loved. I tried never to take for granted the fact that Jake and I were not only both close to our families but that we had them so close to us. They were such big helps when we moved and throughout my illness.

As the holiday season spun into high gear, everyone was busy shopping and decorating. I was so excited to have a house with Jake and to celebrate Christmas together again. Unfortunately, we had a delay right after Thanksgiving that put things on hold for a bit.

Chapter 26

One afternoon while Jake went off to work, I decided to do some finish work around the house. It was some more small painting and odd things that weren't too strenuous for me. Around noon or so, I was painting the trim around the window in our bedroom. I felt myself starting to have a spasm, which had happened on so many times before. As I tried to make my way to my medicine, I collapsed to the floor. I reached to get up but fell backward hitting my head. As I floated in between being asleep and awake, I tried to reach for the phone. The spasm persisted as my body lay convulsing in my own sweat. The last time I had seen the clock it was 12:15. I couldn't remember much of anything after that.

Fortunately around 1:30 Jake had come home to check on me. When he came into the back bedroom, he found me still in spasm on the floor. He could not wake me as my eyes rolled into the back of my head. Struggling to get me to gain consciousness he called 911. When the ambulance arrived, they still could not stop the spasm or wake me from the seizure-like state. I was brought to the hospital once again.

As I was rushed into the emergency room, the doctors struggled to cut off my shirt and bra. Still unconscious, but coming in and out of some state of awake, I felt nothing but the pain in my muscles. My neck, chest, throat, legs and arm again were all contracting in muscle spasms worse than ever. I felt like I was drowning in my own sweat, and I could only suffer to try and ease the pain by putting it out of my head which was hard to do. After several shots again of sedating medicine, the spasm seemed out of anybody's control. My mom, dad, Jake and Laurie were all there by my side. They all tried as desperately as they could to do anything to just take my mind off the pain for a second.

It was not until 2:00 A.M. that my body finally began to give in and rest. My mom spent that night with me in the hospital. I will never forget how happy I was just to awake and see her there sitting in a chair in the corner of the room. I felt like I was seven years old and just needed my mom. Even though she could not fix what was wrong, there is always something about a mother's presence that is more comforting than anything. Jake showed up around 5:00 A.M. to relieve my mother. Even though she left and said she was going home to get some sleep, she was back within two hours, and I knew in my heart she didn't sleep a wink.

Whenever I was in the hospital, my parents and Jake were constantly taking shifts. They were there all the time. At night my room would turn into a busy visiting room with more family and close friends. Jake was amazing…he was there all the time. He would bring little presents, and at night after visiting hours were over, he simply ignored the 8:00 P.M. rule and stayed until I made him leave or simply fell asleep. All the nurses loved him, and he could answer questions about my medications usually better than me. Sometimes he would climb into the bed with me, and we would just lay there for hours. He was my very best friend, and as much as I hated those nights when I could not fall asleep in his arms in our house, he still would try and wait until I was asleep before leaving me for the night.

Even under high doses of sedatives, my body would still spasm on and off throughout the day. It was the first time many people got to see first hand what a real spasm looked like. It was always hard describing what my spasms looked like, and until anyone really saw them first hand, they had no idea what it was I was trying to describe to them. Usually the spasms would be followed by an invasion of nurses who would give me my medication in hopes of stopping the muscles before they became too emerged in a spasm. Sometimes if they were caught early enough, the muscle would relax sooner; but some days it seemed, regardless of the medicines, my body had a mind of its own.

On one day while visiting with my mother and sister Elizabeth, I began having what seemed like a "typical" spasm. However, within moments, things changed drastically. My color drained from my face as my lips turned a blueish color. My eyes were in the back of my head and my entire body was in spasm. The spasm didn't last long, but I was somewhere far away. It was that spasm that actually stopped my heart and breathing.

I have told people that when that happened that day I felt I could hear what was going on. I distinctly remember my mother and sister yelling for me to please just take a breath. Their voices still haunt me to this day. I will never forget the sound of my mother's sadness as the doctors forced her and Elizabeth to leave the room. When they left the room, I could see them in the hallway yelling and crying in desperation for me. I always have a hard time describing this to anyone.

In an effort not to sound crazy, I do remember this and then just like that I awoke in my bed. The small room was crowded with doctors and nurses everywhere and all I saw were the paddles laying next to me on the bed. Luckily, they were able to get me breathing with a shot rather than actually having to use the paddles on me. Still I will never forget that moment in my bed. It was the moment I realized just how serious everything was and I felt afraid. At the same time, while it was happening, I was shockingly at peace. It wasn't until I awoke that my fear ran wildly inside me. I never told anyone but the fear from that day still rests with me and always will. It is a constant reminder of what could have happened if those doctors and nurses had not acted as quickly as they did.

I have often questioned that day and what would have happened had I been home alone? For awhile this was all I thought about but somehow now I just accept the fact that luckily it didn't happen that way. The only thing I ask God now is, "Why did my mother and sister have to be there when it happened?" For me, it is their cries that I will never forget and always hear. With time I have accepted my own answer to that question. It is simply to remind me of how I must keep fighting this disease for the people around me. I realize, had I not heard those cries that day, maybe I would have gone away that day and not come back at all.

The highlight of my hospital visit that stay was the fact that Jake's sister was just a couple floors away, she was having her second child. She had a four year old already and was now adding a second boy to her family. He was born on November 31st. I had the chance to escape my room for a bit to go and see them and even hold the baby. It was amazing to look into his tiny eyes and just feel his life. I had just faced something completely different the day before and now I was able to be so near to someone's life beginning. It was an indescribable feeling. I always admired Jacob's sister. She was a single mom, at twenty-seven, with two kids. Her strength was so inspirational, and I thought she had an incredible way about her. She truly is a great mother and a great person.

When I left the hospital after a week, it was the first time I was not excited to get home. I was scared not to have the doctors and nurses right there for me. Usually I could not wait to leave the hospital but this time I was afraid and hesitant. The doctors took me off many of my medications and tried to concentrate on simply the Lyme antibiotics with some of my other medications too. But they did manage to get me down to only nineteen pills a day rather than the sixty I had been taking prior to that.

During my stay at the hospital, the doctors tried me on an intravenous dose of a different Lyme antibiotic. Many Lyme patients, who have been on the oral antibiotics for some time but still need treatment, will go on the IV because it is said to be a more intense form of treatment that may have quicker results. For myself the particular antibiotic I was given only burned through my veins causing them to become swollen and irritated. For weeks I felt like I could barely use my arms. At one point in the hospital, I had four IV's in, so both my arms were very sore when I got home. I went back on a different antibiotic when I was home but when it began to give me spasms again, I decided to give my body a break and come off the Lyme medicine for the first time in ten months. I had decided my body needed a break through the holidays. I just wanted to enjoy Christmas and New Year's without being completely laid up in bed.

When I got home, I was going to have a visiting nurse who would come twice a week in the beginning and then down to once a week as I became more adjusted. Her name was Julie and she was the sweetest woman I had met. She made my transition home very comfortable. For once I had someone there who would answer my questions and give me feedback on my health. I was so thankful for the time I spent with her. I never hesitated to ask her every question I could think of, and she was never afraid to answer them honestly with me. Even when it came to my emotional disposition, she was a therapist as well as a nurse.

After my time in the hospital, I felt emotionally off balance for reasons I could not exactly pinpoint. Looking back I think I may have just been on an emotional overload but still I felt quiet and lost. My mom and Laurie were great in this area. They were constantly at the house helping to cheer me up. My mom spent every day at my house helping me out. She even helped me decorate my house for Christmas. At first I was just not into it but with time she had me right by her side helping. Over a few days we had transformed my house into a cozy winter wonderland. The soft lights and thoughts of Christmas instantly made me feel better and just happy to be alive.

Jake and I would watch Christmas specials almost every night. We made a gingerbread house, went to Christmas parties, wrapped gifts, went shopping together, decorated our tree, and listened to Christmas music non-stop. I admit we were completely engulfed and over the top with the holiday but it was a great way to take my mind off the hospital. It was a really fun time. I even had Ann, my mom, and my two nieces to my house to make cookies a few days before Christmas. We had so much fun. It was reminding me so much of when I was a little girl and my mom and my sisters and I would be baking for what seemed like an entire day. It was something we always did together, and it was nice to be doing it again only I missed Elizabeth not being there with us. It made me just want to go back in time to when we were all at home together. I think the hardest part of getting older is having to do things without your family or with members of your family missing. As you grow older, everything changes and though some of it may be for the better, it can also be hard to get used to.

I was so used to everyone waking up at my mom and dads house for Christmas and things had not been like that in years. Things were just taking their natural course in life as they do. People grow and you simply cannot ignore that fact. That year, Jake and I went to my parent's for Christmas Eve dinner and to his parent's house for Christmas day dinner. I did insist on spending the night at my parent's so I could have Christmas morning with my mom and dad, though. It was the first year it was just me on Christmas morning, but I had the best time with my parents. It was a Christmas I will never forget because of that.

I knew with the holidays passed the inevitable was staring me in the eyes. It would be only a matter of time before I needed to go back on my Lyme treatment and start focusing on my illness and my recovery. However, I did decide to hold off on that until after I got some second opinions concerning my health at that point in my life.

I had made an appointment in New York City with a specialist who also had treated many people for Lyme Disease. I felt I had a better handle on my body after being off my Lyme medication for some time, and I trusted my Lyme doctor back home so I was less nervous with getting another voice on the subject. There was always that fear of taking a five hour trip to New York to be looked at like I was crazy which had happened so many times before, but luckily that was far from the case.

The doctor in New York was a very well-respected doctor in her field, and though I was intimidated to meet with her, that was instantly gone the moment I sat down in her office. My parents and Jake were with me, and we all felt an instant connection and liking to her. She was well spoken, but not arrogant and had a way of letting me just tell my story without any interruptions. We spent well over an hour with her reliving everything, from my first onset of pain to my hospitalizations and my most recent symptoms.

She followed up my appointment with several blood tests that had never been done. I was amazed there were tests out there that I had never had done, after all I had been a pincushion for the past three years. I knew the ladies at the blood lab as Auntie Beth and Auntie Mel because I was there so much. But I guess that's what a second opinion is best for. It is another way of covering your tracks. The notes following the doctors visit read that I had Stage 3 disseminated chronic Lyme Disease with a possible other tick borne illness along with that. I knew she was still ruling things out and waiting for blood test results but still it was a breath of fresh air to have a second opinion that matched my Lyme doctors back home. I felt a huge sigh of relief.

Things did seem somewhat easier if they had a label on them. Now I at least felt I could use my time getting more knowledgeable about the disease and learn to do things to help me get better. One thing was certain, my road to becoming myself again was just beginning. All my doctors were certain my recovery would take some time and that still wouldn't guarantee me anything. Basically with chronic Lyme Disease the patient will most likely suffer complications from the disease forever. They can also develop other problems due to the disease. I knew the facts and understood what lay ahead but still I felt in my heart I would get better, 100% better. Maybe I was naive, or maybe it was just the competitor that still lived deep within me and begged to come back out, but somehow I felt determined to not be defeated yet again by something out of my control. I decided right then and there that I would always fight my own battle with this disease. I tried not to engulf myself too deep in any websites about Lyme or stories about people who had to change their lives completely around because of chronic Lyme. Instead I engulfed myself in writing my own story, my own book.

The most ongoing and difficult thing for me with Lyme Disease was the constant upward and downward motion of the disease itself. I had so many days when I was okay, and then just like that, I was back in the hospital or being given new medicines. In addition to that, I had so many people who simply didn't believe in my illness. Many of them just weren't educated enough about Lyme disease or they simply thought it was something I had exacerbated in my own mind. As if I enjoyed the idea of being completely incapable of working and taking care of myself. I sometimes felt as if I was trying to prove to people that I was in fact sick and not just using this time to stay in bed and be on "vacation." I always wished the people who felt that way could be there with me when I was throwing up, or having a twenty-two hour long spasm or maybe when my heart stopped completely right in my hospital bed.

It sounds strange but in so many ways I cannot explain the saddening feeling when the ones you love most are just not by your bedside as you lay there in sheer terror. You wake up hoping to see faces that simply aren't there. I was always so grateful to the ones who were there but many times I was left questioning where the others were. Did they not believe me? Was it just denial and they didn't want to see me like this? I never knew.

On so many levels that I will never understand, I wanted people to see the severity of this disease and just exactly what it can do to people. In some altered life, I dreamed that when my heart stopped in the hospital that day that I never came back. I would dream it was just too much and too late to pull me back. I would have only wished something like this to have happened so that my message of Lyme disease could finally be conveyed and maybe even finally spoken. Those lost faces who were not by my bedside would now feel regret as they stood by my casket and wished they had done things differently. If now they could only go back and do things differently. I dreamt that someone would take the honor of finishing my book and publishing it. Maybe it would be then that people would finally see and hear my story told from my heart.

I would ultimately sacrifice myself any day if for one moment people would just stop and listen to my words. If for a moment, they would look a little harder at someone they loved and see inside their own heart. If for a moment, all the mundane nonsense could be put to rest so the innocence and frail beauty of one's character could be seen for exactly what it was. In my case, a 26-year-old girl who loved with all her heart and was driven to fight in all aspects of life because all she really wanted was the one's she loved to see her for who she was, sick but never sad, sick but never dishonest, sick but never doubtful, and mostly sick but always alive. As sad as that story may be, it is an even sadder reality that many people do need this to understand things. They only seem to get it when it is too late. For myself all I really wanted was for the disease to be heard.

Chapter 27

Getting accustomed to the idea of being sick is a constant battle with your emotions. Especially when you are trapped in your home. I lived for the days I would get an escape with my mother, even if it was just as simple as a ride to the beach, it was the time I looked forward to most. I felt my emotions were just riding a wave of confusion that my brain struggled to keep up with.

Every Tuesday our cleaning lady comes to the house. She is a very sweet and honest woman named Maria. At first I would feel awkward and bad being in the house while she was there but she never minded it. After several weeks, I found myself looking forward to seeing her. She was a breath of fresh air in the house. I loved to here her stories of how she came to this country and the struggles she faced when she first came to live here. Somehow it made me realize that there are others out there. When you are in bed for a long time, you have a tendency to forget that the outside world is still functioning.

Maria would sit and talk to me every day I was home. While she cleaned, I laid there listening to her stories. She was a very religious person, and she was always telling me to just pray and somehow God would here my cries. She never failed to tell me how much she also was praying for me. I felt blessed to have such a woman of strong faith have me in her prayers. So I did what she said. I started talking to God more and more each day. I slowly let my anger toward him and my past dissipate and just spoke gently about my life right then, in that moment.

I used to go to church every Sunday and held God very close to my heart, but somewhere in between getting raped, my multiple back surgeries, my lost love and my current illness, I slowly began to close church out of my life. I felt angry with him. I felt I was constantly being tested, and I was simply tired of it. In an effort to figure out my life I also closed the door on my faith. I had never done that before. It was as though I did not know what else to do. I needed someone to be mad at. I knew this theory was all wrong but still it was now "my" only faith I had left.

After meeting my old neighbors, Lucy and Alan, and then with my discussions with Maria, that door I had ignorantly closed on my faith was now slowly opening again. Against my better will, it was really all I had. I realized without my faith I truly had nothing at the base of my heart. I knew I needed to get that aspect of my life back. So each day I would talk to God. I talked to him in a way I had never done before. I let him see my fear, anger and frustration towards him. In an effort to not sound too much like a preacher I just realized it was the one thing missing from my life that I once carried so close to me.

I made a promise to Maria one day when she found me crying in bed. It was the first time I had really let anyone see me just fall apart and be sad. She came into my room with a roll of toilet paper and said, "Good, now you cry." It was like she knew I had been hiding in that bed from everything and everyone. As she left that day, I made a promise to her that I would look at God again and just pray. So that was what I did. I prayed many days with mainly a rambling confusion of thoughts that made no sense. Other days I felt like I was giving a speech on my life and what I wanted to happen. But most days I just talked honestly and directly from my heart. Beyond my questions and anger I just needed to release those thoughts from my head.

In an effort to try and get away from my illness and simply have a change of scenery, Jake had surprised me with a trip down to Florida in early February. I was still off all my Lyme medications and had told all my doctors I wanted to stay off them until I returned from my trip. I wanted to stay on that plateau and be certain my time away would not involve any hospital visits. So with our bags packed and Wrigley at the kennel, we said goodbye to our home for nine days and headed out for Florida.

About four days before we were to leave for Florida, Jake and I had one of our first real fights. Normally our fights lasted minutes because we would start laughing and realize how stupid it was. But that Thursday night was different. Jake's old roommate came by to pick up some of his mail at the house. I always liked him and used to give him the benefit of the doubt on many instances. But this particular night was different.

He started out joking with me, which we did. But later his tone changed as he questioned when the last time I worked was and how this was Jake's house not mine. He continued to belittle me and my illness to the point where I felt tears. I didn't want to cry in front of him, especially him. So I just left the room. The part that angered me more was Jacob just standing there and letting him continue on without coming to my defense. It was the first time I actually felt maybe Jake, too, believed what he was saying. If not, then why wasn't he saying something to make him stop?

Jake had been so supportive through everything, but when I needed him most he was not there. I felt so hurt and saddened by his lack of actions. I felt more lost in that moment of time than I had ever felt before with him. I knew guys had that way of doing that in front of their friends because I had experienced it so many times before but never with Jake, he just wasn't like that. I sat silently in the other room wondering where he had been in that moment.

I started to think about the hospital and my heart stopping and those spasms that lasted fourteen hours long, I wished his old roommate could have been there to see that. He was the exact reason I needed to write and tell about this disease. It was people just like him that night that needed to see first hand what can happen. The only difficult thing was that everything I was feeling toward him I was now in that instant feeling toward Jake. I told him he was no better than him. The problem was I didn't love Jake's roommate so I didn't really care what he thought deep down, what bothered me more is that Jake was not there for me.

After questioning him on this, he had no real answer for me. He just felt so bad he could have hurt me in a way like that. His eyes were filled with tears as he looked at me and wondered where he was for me in that moment. We fought for the first time in a while. It was weird fighting with him, I felt lost. I think it was because it hadn't happened that much. I told him to never let it happen again and that was it. From his eyes I could tell he was deeply and sincerely sorry for his lack of action so we put it aside and talked about our trip and how much fun we would have together.

The whole plane ride I was excited like a child. I couldn't wait to get there and be away from everything at home. I knew both Jake and I were in need of a mental vacation from all we had been going through back at home. Even though I knew what remained at home for me upon my return would be a difficult road to face, I tried desperately to leave that in the airport back in Massachusetts so I could simply fly away from it all. And that was exactly what we did. We boarded that plane with our hearts and love for one another and left everything else tucked away until we needed to come home.

When we arrived at his parent's home, we wasted no time in getting on the boat to catch that nights sunset. The year before Jake had always said his best memory of me was when I saw live dolphins for the first time. He said I ran around like a kid as excited as ever. He always told me that was the highlight of his whole trip. He had never seen anyone get so excited over dolphins in his life. He only hoped that first night I would see the dolphins again. Though his doubts of us running into any dolphins on that first night were deep, his doubts were changed the moment I rose from the boat in excitement upon my first dolphin sighting. I had told Jake that night that I was certain we would see those dolphins, and though he thought there was a greater chance we wouldn't, we did. Somehow I just knew. Like the year before I felt free the moment I saw those beautiful creatures before me. Their ability to swim with such grace, it always intrigued me.

The ocean always intrigued me though. Maybe it was from my childhood and growing up so close to the water. I don't know, though, I think regardless the ocean would always fascinate me. When I looked at it, I wondered about all the life that existed beneath it. All of the world that remained so alive covered by this enormous blanket for only the truly interested to investigate. The rest of us remain above this blanket simply fantasizing about what lies deep beneath.

For myself I wanted nothing more than for someday to dive deep down into that great ocean of life and live among it. I wanted to dance among the stars then just like that fly deep into the ocean swimming as fast as I could breathing in all the life and then shooting out of the water and flying back towards the clouds and dancing again among the skies. Every time I see the ocean, I imagine myself someday living that fantasy. Escaping all that exists to simply hide beneath that blanket just for a moment.

After watching those dolphins swim for a while, Jake and I sat and watched the sun set peacefully on the horizon. With nothing but the ocean before us it was as though the sun just melted into the water. It was beautiful and reminded me of just how much I loved being alive. I was in paradise with my sweetheart and just enjoying every minute of our time together. I was escaping my thoughts of being sick and focusing on my time without those poisonous medications that I would return to.

Although we always imagine all vacations to be perfect, that is not always the case. Somehow miles away from home and "reality", one day Jake and I got caught up in talking about our life together and decisions we needed to make. The discussion took a crash landing on us getting married and where we stood with our next step in life. I had always told Jake I hated the idea of us living together without being engaged or married, and somehow, that day, it came up in conversation. He told me that he had never planned to be living with me that long without being engaged but things had changed. He said though everything in his heart was ready to ask me to marry him, he was fearful of me. He told me he had too many fears that I was not in the same place as him. For the first time, he pointed out to me the things I was saying that led him to believe I was not ready to marry him.

I never realized what I had been saying but perhaps it was true, maybe Jake was right. The things I so blindly was saying to him were simply words I was saying from my heart that I didn't even pay attention to. Maybe he was right...maybe I was not ready to get married at all. Suddenly I was mortified by all I had been saying. I remembered where he was getting these ideas from, and they were straight from my own mouth.

You never plan to have these deep discussions while on vacation, but lets face it, you cannot always plan the timing of things. It would be a lot easier if somehow we could. It was on our vacation that I realized just what I had been saying to Jake all along. I was telling him how I wanted to be able to take care of myself before I let anyone else really take care of me. I also told him how I wished I was healthy so that I could go and do all that I wished I could be doing. I will never know how these words of mine may have hurt him and his simple dreams of us being together forever. Instead I was just stating my own thoughts to my best friend. What I didn't realize was all along all he really wanted was for us to take care of each other.

Although I felt bad for what I had been saying, I was also starting to think that maybe if these were my thoughts, maybe they were really just my truth in my life right then. Maybe I wasn't ready to get married and maybe I did need to stop worrying so much about it. I suppose I was the naive one who thought maybe on that trip Jake and I would be coming home engaged. But instead we just came home. We came home to our house and to our fate...dealing with the inevitable.

Chapter 28

When we came home from Florida, it was time for me to start focusing back on my health. I had spent close to two months off my medication and living on that plateau. Now the time had come when I would dive head first off that plateau and into my health.

It was the day after I returned home from my trip that I began my Lyme medication again. That very same night I also received a call that changed my life. It was my doctor from New York. She had sent my Lyme tests out to a well-known laboratory to do more sophisticated testing. They used the Western Blot which is a more in depth study of the lab work than what had been done before. This was the first time I had the Western Blot test done and normally it is the best indicator of a patient and if they do in fact have Lyme disease. I was relieved when the doctor confirmed that I did in fact have Lyme disease. My tests came back positive six times, so this time I knew for sure.

When I hung up the phone with her, I wasted no time in calling my mom and dad to tell them the news. It was a bittersweet moment. I was so happy to finally have a second positive diagnosis and to actually know now what I was fighting. My mom answered the phone and responded to the news with tears of both relief and sadness. I knew she was so happy to finally know what I had and that her fear of all those other diseases was now out of the picture and put to rest. We all knew my road to recovery from that moment was going to be long and grueling. I knew my mother was sad for the fact that she had begged so hard for the doctors to test and treat me for Lyme Disease two years earlier. There was no denying that the sooner I had been treated the better chances for a full recovery. I was now dealing with a much more intense case of Lyme that would need a longer period of time for recovery. But still the agony of simply not knowing was now gone, so we basked in the lightness of that for the time at hand.

As soon as I started my medications, I was feeling the effects of the disease all throughout my body. It was all too familiar. The muscle cramps and spasms, and the nausea and migraine headaches that left me paralyzed in pain. I was back in bed, an all too familiar place that I did not want to be. I could not help but wish that Jake and I could have just stayed in Florida. It was there that I was able to hide from all of this and just not deal with it. Though I was not getting better, I was not feeling my body slip away from me in the way it was now.

Nobody can really explain the effects of Lyme disease on a patient because each person and patient is different. Some experience more mild symptoms and others suffer the effects of the disease for the rest of their lives. I felt driven to fight and wanted to face my health head on and just beat it. I was faced yet again with another challenge, and this one I was determined to beat no matter what it took.

My mind was also now consumed with all those doctors out there who did not believe in my illness. The ones who thought I simply had a psychological disorder and was manifesting all of my stress in this way. I thought about all the times I was rushed to the emergency room only to be told I was having a panic attack, then shot up with some morphine, and sent on my way. I remembered the doctors who interrogated me on drugs and repeatedly questioned what drugs I was using that were causing this in my body. I thought about everyone who thought I was suffering from posttraumatic stress syndrome from being raped. I wondered how nobody took the time to listen to me. I had merely one doctor, my Lyme doctor, who stood by my side through everything and never made me feel crazy. I held onto his knowledge about this disease and his faith in getting me well. He was the only one I felt I could trust in the medical community at that point. I felt blessed to now know what I had and to have more doctors fighting in my corner.

With every day that passed, my body grew more and more tired from the disease. I was weak and feeling beaten. I felt my body was being invaded by something that did not belong. I grew angry at the disease. I felt that, now that I knew what I had, I could barely believe that it had caused such destruction in my body. As I lay in bed day in and day out, the thoughts ran loosely in my head. I had nothing else to do but think.

Here I was, again, back in bed trying to recover. It was all too familiar a feeling. Only this time I did not know what to look ahead to. I wanted a goal to reach towards. When I had my back surgeries and was in bed, I dreamed of finishing school. I needed something like that to reach for. I was already living in a great home with a great man beside me.

But somehow I needed to reach for more. I needed to want something else. Mostly I wanted my life back. But somewhere between laying in bed and dreaming of getting well, I came to the realization that maybe this was my job to handle. I felt maybe there was a reason I was sick. Maybe it was so I could help others out there. I wanted to make a statement about Lyme Disease, I wanted people to really see what it could do to the body, I wanted to tell this story of my life.

I knew I had so much to share with people. I had a story to tell and all I dreamed of was someone to tell it to. My motivation came in many forms but one day it came from my four year old niece. She came over to visit me in bed, which she did a lot. We would sit and watch show after show on Nickelodeon and Disney. I loved her company. Sometimes we would color or other times she would just talk to me. I felt like I was talking to someone much older, but at the same time I was able to talk about the most mundane things. She would tell me about school and things she loved most about her teacher and her friends. In those hours I spent with her, I always seemed to ignore the pain that ran so deep in my skin. It just disappeared.

After she left one day, she went to my mom's for dinner. At the table she said to my mother that she had a very special wish she wanted to make. She wanted to make my legs better. She wanted me to walk again. I could not help but feel sad when I heard that story. It was the first time I realized she actually saw me as sick. Before I don't think it ever phased her or me but that day something was different, she saw me for who I was and what was happening to me. Her little heart just wanted me to get better. She had more compassion in that four-year-old heart of hers than many people I knew. I knew I had to make that wish of hers come true. I made it my goal to do that for her. She was my motivation. How amazing a child is. How amazing the power they hold and the truth they see. When we think they are too little to understand, somehow they amaze us with their ability to take in what is real. I didn't know much about my health and where things were going but I did know one thing, I would never let my niece down. With her wish in my heart and my anger in mind, I was determined to fight this disease with all the strength I had. With my efforts on keeping that goal in sight I began keeping my promise. I took out an old journal of mine that I had written the "likeness" of a book in and read it.

It was something I had wrote back in the fall before John came to live on the Cape. I remember starting to write just to write and before I knew it I had filled every page in that journal with a story. A story about my life.

I went back and read every page of it. I threw myself into the past, reliving each and every experience all over again. After I finished reading each page, I sat down and began typing. Every thought in my mind began to emerge from my brain. I couldn't stop. All those walks I had taken and mentally written my life in my head were now being put onto paper. I had no idea what my intentions of writing were I just knew I had something to say, a story to tell, and I wanted it to be heard.

I began to think of myself as one of those people who goes through experiences in life not because she is dealt a bad hand but because she is supposed to do something about it. I wanted to use each and every moment in my life that had tested me up to that point to help anyone else out there who was listening. At first I used my writing as the most sane form of therapy. It allowed me to talk out loud with no ridicule or remarks. It was just my most pure and honest thoughts I had in my heart that I needed to get out. What started as therapy became my "book" that I wanted to share with people. It was the best medicine for me. Writing about my life allowed me to escape everything I was going through at that point. It was a chance to take my focus off how horrible I was feeling and the pain my body was enduring. I spent my days in bed with my laptop in front of me. In many ways it became my job. So with that in mind I knew I needed to "work" just as hard as I would any other job. Because this was now my own set mission in life.

I thought back to one of my favorite English professors in college and his final words to me. He had told me to write. No matter what I was doing and where I was going to just keep writing. He told me I had a way of reaching people with my words. At the time I took his advice and put it in my back pocket. For some time I had forgotten about it. It wasn't until I started to write again that his words were alive in my heart. I had forgotten who I was without writing. I had always written, but until then, it was always just words that only I read. Now I had such a greater audience I wanted to touch. In so many ways I had been lost without doing something that I had always done. To be writing again gave me a sense of strength that no medicine could have ever given me. It made me feel alive in a way that I hadn't felt in a long time.

In a lot of ways I had always been writing my life. I had always been telling my story aloud in my head. I suppose I never thought I would be writing my story for others to read. But knowing I could help others out there, inspired me in ways I never knew I was capable of. When I was not busy writing, I was simply in bed wishing and hoping for the day I would walk out into the world and once again feel like myself all over. Almost like being reborn into the world but now with life's lessons behind me.

I had been sick for so long that I had forgotten what a state of feeling good felt like. Both of my Lyme doctors had thought that there may have even been the possibility my body had been infected with the disease even longer than we had anticipated. They felt I had really had this horrible disease for much longer than three years. In a lot of ways it made perfect sense. I had really felt sick and hid it for quite some time prior to all of this coming out so maybe they were right. All I knew was it made me feel a little bit more sad and a little bit less crazy. It finally all started to make sense. Still I was angry and sad at the fact that so many years of my life were being taken by this disease. I wished I could get those years back. That was the hardest part, knowing something could actually take away part of your life in such a way. I was twenty-six, but I actually wanted to feel it.

When the news arrived that I did in fact have Lyme disease, I had yet another decision to make. I was taking the oral antibiotics at that point and was confined to my bed most days because my muscles were just shutting down in my legs. It was a weakness I had felt so many times before, I just always hoped it would never actually come back. Still I needed to think clearly in order to make my next decision about regarding my treatment options.

My Lyme doctor on the Cape suggested I continue on the oral antibiotics for another eight months or so. He felt it was the best route for me to take. He was hesitant to start an IV treatment with me at that point in time. He felt it was just too soon. However, the doctor I saw in New York was saying just the opposite, She felt it was time for me to begin treatment with the IV and come off the oral antibiotics all together. My primary care physician and my neurologist also felt the IV was the next step for me. So with faith in my heart, I followed the majority vote and made it my personal decision to go on the IV antibiotics.

I figured at that point nothing else mattered, it couldn't get much worse and if it did, I was ready to fight anything. I felt empowered for the first time during my sickness to finally make the ultimate decision in the end. I needed to have my say in something. I had felt like, up to that point in this whole process, I was just a puppet doing whatever the doctors told me to do. It was now I knew I needed to take a stand and take control of how I wanted to go about fighting off this horrible disease. It was as though my body was being violated and taken over by something that did not belong. I wanted to walk again, I wanted to fight, I wanted to feel healthy, and most importantly I wanted a chance to live again, I wanted to feel alive. I didn't know at that point if I had made the right decision, and I knew I probably wouldn't know for a while. But I knew for once I had decided that with getting better my goal and having my family and my soul mate to support me, I felt if I fell, I would indefinitely be caught. So I leapt with all my heart and closed my eyes hoping to awake to a brighter day.

Chapter 29

Perhaps the most challenging aspect while traveling among our oceans of time is seeing what lay's ahead, what breaks upon the horizon and allowing yourself to see the future that we have traveled so far to reach. For myself this had been an obstacle that has thwarted itself constantly in my plain vision. As many waves that I sail through and beyond, I still struggle to see where my ship is voyaging. Guided merely by that wind that casts my sails forth, I feel as though I am floating so quickly with no end in sight. People say, "The journey's the thing," but I find no peace in that assertion. Though I try to live by its grace I find no hope in the moments that the journey seems to take you nowhere. The moment your ship is steered in a manner that seems unworthy to your life.

My journey has been one of pain, heartache, fear and hardship. Though I try and bask in the many moments of intimacy, happiness, sunshine and joy; it always seems to end in some water that I fear so badly to sail upon. I suppose there is a God somewhere who feels these challenges are merely the struggles all people must face in order to combat the fear they may encounter. I agree. Challenge me but please show me why. Show me the reason. I have begged all my life for one fleeting moment where I can venture to say, "thank you" now I know the reason I was faced with such a challenge. But I know those reasons will never be revealed to me so I try to continue my journey without waiting for them.

People will say life can close one door only to open a window but who chooses to open that window, should it be me? This is the conclusion or question that I feel has been presented to me. Maybe my time has come to open my own window, create my own fate, and begin to live and accept my own life. I want to take one last breath, close the door behind me, and sail towards the horizon. Free of all my burdens, I am ready to live for me and begin my journey through this clouded ocean until I find what it is I have so valiantly searched for. Horizons are the lives we create for ourselves driven from the desire to move forth from our past and overcome those who have held our wings down.

The greatest thing about the ocean is that you can see forever; it seems no matter how far you stretch your vision you can never really see the end. Maybe it is because we know deep in our mind that there really is no end. Life is one continuous circle that has no real beginning or end to it.

We know of birth and we know of death but there is still all the uncertainty in the middle. The choices we are bound to make that bring us to where we are and make us each different from the next. In all my life thus far the thing I have feared over and over is that of living a simple routine life that people have a tendency to fall into unknowingly. Being predictable. Living a life with no spontaneity or vicariously relishing in the stories others tell you.

I have always set one goal for myself that I constantly try to embrace. Live each minute of every day as if it were the first day. Some would disagree with this and say I should live each day as if it were the last. I don't like that. I do not want to live with the thought in mind that death is closer than birth. I like it better the other way around, seeing my birth into this amazing world each and every day. By choosing to live in this manner then I do not take what I see for granted. I can look and embrace things like a child and see with grandeur and admiration. If you ever really watch a child who sees a sunset for the first time, you can see a peace and joy that seems to light up their face. A simple sunset, something we can see every day if we want, yet they look at it with such amazement.

I remember the very first time I saw the sun set. It was a warm summer night, and I was with my family at the beach near our house. I was sitting in my mother's lap as the sky began to turn every shade of red, orange and yellow until the clouds overhead appeared to be on fire. As the sun slowly melted beneath the horizon, I felt sadness and began to cry. I told my mom I was afraid the sun would never come back again. As she comforted me, I knew through her voice that everything would be fine. I have seen thousands upon thousands of sunsets since then, and I have grown to appreciate them through those same child-like eyes, almost as if I was seeing it again for the first time. I never miss an opportunity to see the sun rest on the horizon for, some reason like my mother's voice that night, it just makes me feel like somehow everything is going to be okay.

I have told people that story and it still makes me feel calm inside, I suppose that is why I will continue to live by its word. The horizon is just the place I turn to when I feel I need some solace in this crazy world. As I look upon the horizon today, it seems a bit hazy and difficult to see in the distance. I can see the faint resemblance of a destination somewhere out there though I am just not quite sure in which direction and what waters it does lay among.

So now I hope to just appreciate the moment because my next adventure calls from that hazy distance and I must face those waters to find it. I pray that within those waters I find peace, health and happiness. As I board my ship I am no longer facing this on my own. Beside me resides my family, friends and my soul mate. Love and faith will carry my sails somewhere, and though I do not know where, I know I have those around me to lean on. I know I have taken chances, faced my fears, embraced happiness, and fallen deeply in love. With that in hand I am ready for whatever the ocean may present to me, but most of all I am living. I will not give up here and accept my fate. I will search and fight those waters until I find my health and am left simply to love.

Epilog

All my life I have been running, in many ways that can be said in both a literal and physical sense. As a child it was more physical but as I have grown it has been more literal. I have been running from many things in my life. I run as fast as I can in hopes to escape the deep fear of being hurt, being betrayed, taken advantage of, and heartbroken. Through all the moments I have been running I have come to realize one factor that remains a constant. Love.

Though I have tried desperately to run from love, I have grown to realize, when you do in fact find it, you can never run from it. You can only learn to surrender to it. Which I have. My dear Jacob, my best friend, my love and my heart. I am so lucky to have found such a man in my life. My life has taken me down many paths and many hardships but if it hadn't, it would have never led me straight into the arms of my love. So I have learned, rather than being angry for the challenges I have faced in life, to be thankful and to be grateful. For if it was not for each and every one of these moments in my life, I may not have had this man who comes home to me every day. A man who regardless of all that has been put before him has done nothing but loved me in ways I never knew possible. For that I am truly lucky.

So now here I am. I may not know exactly what does remain around the next corner, but I do know I am ready to face whatever that challenge may be. I am left with questions about my health and if I will ever actually walk or run again. I have no answers for that or where this disease may take me. All I truly know is that I have made decisions to begin my process towards a recovery and hopefully regaining many aspects of my life back that I have lost over these several years. I am hopeful to awaken that athlete inside me that resides deep in my soul but has been unwillingly silenced due to my inabilities.

I want to compete again. I want to feel the excitement of a victory and the feeling of putting all I have inside me on the line. It is with this mentality that I will defeat my challenges with this disease and know deep in my heart that someday I will walk again, and this time I will be walking each step with a little more grace and a little more appreciation.

Through all the time I spent writing, Jake was really the only person who I allowed to hear any of my book in great length. Every so often we would lay in bed together and I would read him chapters from my "life." He was my best audience, a critic but also a fan. I loved him for that. I feared in my heart that maybe he would hate hearing about things from my past, especially when it involved love. But that faded when I realized my book may have began with someone else but it ended with him. One time after I had finished reading a passage he asked me when I began writing my book. It was a simple question with an even simpler answer, I told him it was, "While I was walking."

Kis. Mclaron@gmail

CPSIA information can be obtained at www.ICGtesting.com
Printed in the USA
LVOW12s2055190314

378099LV00001B/34/P

9 781424 158188